Jean Webster

ALICE JANE CHANDLER (Jean Webster) was born in Fredonia, New York, on July 24, 1876, into a family that shared her delight in writing and her buoyant sense of humor. Her father was a publisher and a business partner of her mother's cousin, Samuel Clemens. Jean Webster was named Jane after Clemens's mother.

While still a student at Vassar College, Jean Webster wrote for the Poughkeepsie newspaper. Her investigation of homes for orphaned or delinquent children convinced her that adversity need not prevent success. She expressed this with lively humor and compassion in her novel *Daddy-Long-Legs*, published in 1912. It was an instant hit. She adapted the novel into a four-act dramatic play. It then became a silent movie for Mary Pickford and was later produced as a musical play. There were two other films: one, in 1931, starred Janet Gaynor, and the other, in 1955, featured Leslie Caron and Fred Astaire in the leading roles. There was, of course, a sequel, and in 1915 *Dear Enemy* continued the saga of the orphans at the John Grier Home.

Jean Webster also wrote *When Patty Went to College*, based on her Vassar classmate, the poet Adelaide Crapsey; *The Wheat Princess; Jerry Junior; The Four Pools Mystery; Much Ado About Peter;* and *Just Patty.*

Jean Webster married Glenn Ford McKinney in 1915. They lived in New York City and had a small farm in Massachusetts, where they raised ducks and pheasants.

Jean Webster died in 1916, following the birth of her daughter.

YEARLING CLASSICS

Works of lasting literary merit
by classic international writers

YEARLING BOOKS/YOUNG YEARLINGS/YEARLING CLASSICS are designed especially to entertain and enlighten young people. Patricia Reilly Giff, consultant to this series, received the bachelor's degree from Marymount College. She holds the master's degree in history from St. John's University, and a Professional Diploma in Reading from Hofstra University. She was a teacher and reading consultant for many years, and is the author of numerous books for young readers.

For a complete listing of all Yearling titles, write to
Dell Readers Service, P.O. Box 1045,
South Holland, IL 60473.

Dear Enemy

Jean Webster

Published by
Dell Publishing
a division of
Bantam Doubleday Dell Publishing Group, Inc.
666 Fifth Avenue
New York, New York 10103

The trademark Yearling® is registered in the U.S. Patent and
Trademark Office.
The trademark Dell® is registered in the U.S. Patent and Trade-
mark Office.

ISBN: 0-440-40440-1

Printed in the United States of America

April 1991

10 9 8 7 6 5 4 3 2 1

OPM

Dear Enemy

Dear Judy:

Your letter is here. I have read it twice, and with
amazement. Do I understand that Jervis has given you, for
a Christmas present, the making over of the John Grier
Home into a model institution, and that you have chosen
me to disburse the money? Me—I, Sallie McBride, the
head of an orphan-asylum! My poor people, have you lost
your senses, or have you become addicted to the use of
opium, and is this the raving of two fevered imaginations?
I am exactly as well fitted to take care of one hundred
children as to become the curator of a zoo.

And you offer as bait an interesting Scotch doctor? My
dear Judy,—likewise my dear Jervis,—I see through you! I
know exactly the kind of family conference that has been
held about the Pendleton fireside.

"Isn't it a pity that Sallie hasn't amounted to more
since she left college? She ought to be doing something
useful instead of frittering her time away in the petty
social life of Worcester. Also [Jervis speaks] she is getting interested in that confounded young Hallock, too
good-looking and fascinating and erratic; I never did like
politicians. We must deflect her mind with some uplifting
and absorbing occupation until the danger is past. Ha! I
have it! We will put her in charge of the John Grier
Home."

Oh, I can hear him as clearly as if I were there! On the
occasion of my last visit in your delectable household

1

Jervis and I had a very solemn conversation in regard to (1) marriage, (2) the low ideals of politicians, (3) the frivolous, useless lives that society women lead.

Please tell your moral husband that I took his words deeply to heart, and that ever since my return to Worcester I have been spending one afternoon a week reading poetry with the inmates of the Female Inebriate Asylum. My life is not so purposeless as it appears.

Also let me assure you that the politician is not dangerously imminent; and that, anyway, he is a very desirable politician, even though his views on tariff and single tax and trade-unionism do not exactly coincide with Jervis's.

Your desire to dedicate my life to the public good is very sweet, but you should look at it from the asylum's point of view. Have you no pity for those poor defenseless little orphan children?

I have, if you haven't, and I respectfully decline the position which you offer.

I shall be charmed, however, to accept your invitation to visit you in New York, though I must acknowledge that I am not very excited over the list of gaieties you have planned.

Please substitute for the New York Orphanage and the Foundling Hospital a few theaters and operas and a dinner or so. I have two new evening gowns and a blue and gold coat with a white fur collar.

I dash to pack them; so telegraph fast if you don't wish to see me for myself alone, but only as a successor to Mrs. Lippett.

> Yours as ever,
> Entirely frivolous,
> And intending to remain so,
> SALLIE McBRIDE.

P.S. Your invitation is especially seasonable. A charming young politician named Gordon Hallock is to be in New York next week. I am sure you will like him when you know him better.

P.S. 2. Sally taking her afternoon walk as Judy would like to see her:

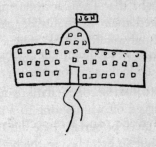

I ask you again, have you both gone mad?

THE JOHN GRIER HOME,
February 15.

Dear Judy:

We arrived in a snow-storm at eleven last night, Singapore and Jane and I. It does not appear to be customary for superintendents of orphan-asylums to bring with them personal maids and Chinese chows. The night-watchman and house-keeper, who had waited up to receive me, were thrown into an awful flutter. They had never seen the like of Sing, and thought that I was introducing a wolf into the fold. I reassured them as to his dogginess; and the watchman, after studying his black tongue, ventured a witticism. He wanted to know if I fed him on huckleberry pie.

It was difficult to find accommodations for my family. Poor Sing was dragged off whimpering to a strange woodshed, and given a piece of burlap. Jane did not fare much better. There was not an extra bed in the building, barring a five-foot crib in the hospital room. She, as you know, approaches six. We tucked her in, and she spent the night folded up like a jackknife. She has limped about to-day, looking like a decrepit letter S, openly deploring this latest escapade on the part of her flighty mistress, and longing for the time when we shall come to our senses, and return to the parental fireside in Worcester.

I know that she is going to spoil all my chances of being popular with the rest of the staff. Having her here is the silliest idea that was ever conceived; but you know my family. I fought their objections step by step, but they made their last stand on Jane. If I brought her along to see that I ate nourishing food and didn't stay up all night, I

4

might come—temporarily; but if I refused to bring her—oh, dear me, I am not sure that I was ever again to cross the threshold of Stone Gate! So here we are, and neither of us very welcome, I am afraid.

I woke by a gong at six this morning, and lay for a time listening to the racket that twenty-five little girls made in the lavatory over my head. It appears that they do not get baths,—just face-washes,—but they make as much splashing as twenty-five puppies in a pool. I rose and dressed and explored a bit. You were wise in not having me come to look the place over before I engaged.

While my little charges were at breakfast, it seemed a happy time to introduce myself; so I sought the dining-room. Horror piled on horror—those bare drab walls and oil-cloth-covered tables with tin cups and plates and wooden benches, and, by way of decoration, that one illuminated text, "The Lord Will Provide"! The trustee who added that last touch must possess a grim sense of humor.

Really, Judy, I never knew there was any spot in the world so entirely ugly; and when I saw those rows and rows of pale, listless, blue-uniformed children, the whole dismal business suddenly struck me with such a shock that I almost collapsed. It seemed like an unachievable goal for one person to bring sunshine to one hundred little faces when what they need is a mother apiece.

I plunged into this thing lightly enough, partly because you were too persuasive, and mostly, I honestly think, because that scurrilous Gordon Hallock laughed so uproariously at the idea of my being able to manage an asylum. Between you all you hypnotized me. And then of course, after I began reading up on the subject and visiting all those seventeen institutions, I got excited over orphans,

and wanted to put my own ideas into practice. But now
I'm aghast at finding myself here; it's such a stupendous
undertaking. The future health and happiness of a hundred human beings lie in my hands, to say nothing of their
three or four hundred children and thousand grandchil-
dren. The thing's geometrically progressive. It's awful.
Who am I to undertake this job? Look, oh, look for
another superintendent!

Jane says dinner's ready. Having eaten two of your
institution meals, the thought of another doesn't excite
me.

LATER.

The staff had mutton hash and spinach, with tapioca
pudding for dessert; what the children had I hate to
consider.

I started to tell you about my first official speech at
breakfast this morning. It dealt with all the wonderful new
changes that are to come to the John Grier Home through
the generosity of Mr. Jervis Pendleton, the president of
our board of trustees, and of Mrs. Pendleton, the dear
"Aunt Judy" of every little boy and girl here.

Please don't object to my featuring the Pendleton family
so prominently. I did it for political reasons. As the entire
working-staff of the institution was present, I thought it a
good opportunity to emphasize the fact that all of these
upsetting innovations come straight from headquarters,
and not out of my excitable brain.

The children stopped eating and stared. The conspicuous
color of my hair and the frivolous tilt of my nose are
evidently new attributes in a superintendent. My col-

leagues also showed plainly that they consider me too young and too inexperienced to be set in authority. I haven't seen Jervis's wonderful Scotch doctor yet, but I assure you that he will have to be *very* wonderful to make up for the rest of these people, especially the kindergarten teacher. Miss Snaith and I clashed early on the subject of fresh air; but I intend to get rid of this dreadful institution smell, if I freeze every child into a little ice statue.

This being a sunny, sparkling, snowy afternoon, I ordered that dungeon of a playroom closed and the children out of doors.

"She's chasin' us out," I heard one small urchin grumbling as he struggled into a two-years-too-small overcoat.

They simply stood about the yard, all humped in their clothes, waiting patiently to be allowed to come back in. No running or shouting or coasting or snowballs. Think of it! These children don't know how to play.

STILL LATER.

I have already begun the congenial task of spending your money. I bought eleven hot-water bottles this afternoon (every one that the village drug store contained) likewise some woolen blankets and padded quilts. And the windows are wide open in the babies' dormitory. Those poor little tots are going to enjoy the perfectly new sensation of being able to breathe at night.

There are a million things I want to grumble about, but it's half-past ten, and Jane says I *must* go to bed.

Yours in command,
SALLIE McBRIDE.

P.S. Before turning in, I tiptoed through the corridor to make sure that all was right, and what do you think I found? Miss Snaith softly closing the windows in the babies' dormitory! Just as soon as I can find a suitable position for her in an old ladies' home, I am going to discharge that woman.

Jane takes the pen from my hand.

Good night.

Dear Judy:

Dr. Robin MacRae called this afternoon to make the acquaintance of the new superintendent. Please invite him to dinner upon the occasion of his next visit to New York, and see for yourself what your husband has done. Jervis grossly misrepresented the facts when he led me to believe that one of the chief advantages of my position would be the daily intercourse with a man of Dr. MacRae's polish and brilliancy and Scholarliness and charm.

He is tall and thinnish, with sandy hair and cold gray eyes. During the hour he spent in my society (and I was very sprightly) no shadow of a smile so much as lightened the straight line of his mouth. Can a shadow lighten? Maybe not; but, anyway, what *is* the matter with the man? Has he committed some remorseful crime, or is his taciturnity due merely to his natural Scotchness? He's as companionable as a granite tombstone!

Incidentally, our doctor didn't like me any more than I liked him. He thinks I'm frivolous and inconsequential, and totally unfitted for this position of trust. I dare say Jervis has had a letter from him by now asking to have me removed.

In the matter of conversation we didn't hit it off in the least. He discussed broadly and philosophically the evils of institutional care for dependent children, while I lightly deplored the unbecoming coiffure that prevails among our girls.

To prove my point, I had in Sadie Kate, my special

9

errand orphan. Her hair is strained back as tightly as
though it had been done with a monkey-wrench, and is
braided behind into two wiry little pigtails. Decidedly,
orphans' ears need to be softened. But Dr. Robin MacRae
doesn't give a hang whether their ears are becoming or
not; what he cares about is their stomachs. We also split
upon the subject of red petticoats. I don't see how any
little girl can preserve any self-respect when dressed in a
red flannel petticoat an irregular inch longer than her blue
checked gingham dress; but he thinks that red petticoats
are cheerful and warm and hygienic. I foresee a warlike
reign for the new superintendent.

In regard to the doctor, there is just one detail to be
thankful for: he is almost as new as I am, and he cannot
instruct me in the traditions of the asylum. I don't believe
I *could* have worked with the old doctor, who, judging
from the specimens of his art that he left behind, knew as
much about babies as a veterinary surgeon.

In the matter of asylum etiquette, the entire staff has
undertaken my education. Even the cook this morning
told me firmly that the John Grier Home has cornmeal
mush on Wednesday nights.

Are you searching hard for another superintendent? I'll
stay until she comes, but please find her fast.

Yours,

With my mind made up,

SALLIE MCBRIDE.

SUP'T'S OFFICE,
JOHN GRIER HOME,
February 21.

Dear Gordon:

Are you still insulted because I wouldn't take your advice? Don't you know that a reddish-haired person of Irish forebears, with a dash of Scotch, can't be driven, but must be gently led? Had you been less obnoxiously insistent, I should have listened sweetly, and been saved. As it is, I frankly confess that I have spent the last five days in repenting our quarrel. You were right, and I was wrong, and, as you see, I handsomely acknowledge it. If I ever emerge from this present predicament, I shall in the future be guided (almost always) by your judgment. Could any woman make a more sweeping retraction than that?

The romantic glamour which Judy cast over this orphan-asylum exists only in her poetic imagination. The place is *awful.* Words can't tell you how dreary and dismal and smelly it is: long corridors, bare walls; blue-uniformed, dough-faced little inmates that haven't the slightest resemblance to human children. And oh, the dreadful institution smell! A mingling of wet scrubbed floors, unaired rooms, and food for a hundred people always steaming on the stove.

The asylum not only has to be made over, but every child as well, and it's too herculean a task for such a selfish, luxurious, and lazy person as Sallie McBride ever to have undertaken. I'm resigning the very first moment that Judy can find a suitable successor; but that, I fear, will not be immediately. She has gone off South, leaving

11

me stranded; and of course, after having promised, I can't simply abandon her asylum. But in the meantime I assure you that I'm homesick.

Write me a cheering letter, and send a flower to brighten my private drawing-room. I inherited it, furnished, from Mrs. Lippett. The wall is covered with a tapestry paper in brown and red; the furniture is electric-blue plush, except the center-table, which is gilt. Green predominates in the carpet. If you presented some pink rosebuds, they would complete the color scheme.

I really was obnoxious that last evening, but you are avenged.

Remorsefully yours,
SALLIE MCBRIDE.

P.S. You needn't have been so grumpy about the Scotch doctor. The man is everything dour that the word "Scotch" implies. I detest him on sight, and he detests me. Oh, we're going to have a sweet time working together!

U.S. CAPITOL

JOHN GRIER HOME

Red Hair

"Oh Willow Woe is me
Alack & Well a day
If I were only free
I'd hie me far away"

My dear Gordon:

Your vigorous and expensive message is here. I know that you have plenty of money, but that is no reason why you should waste it so frivolously. When you feel so bursting with talk that only a hundred-word telegram will relieve an explosion, at least turn it into a night lettergram. My orphans can use the money if you don't need it.

Also, my dear sir, please use a trifle of common sense. Of course I can't chuck the asylum in the casual manner you suggest. It wouldn't be fair to Judy and Jervis. If you will pardon the statement, they have been my friends for many more years than you, and I have no intention of letting them go hang. I came up here in a spirit of—well, say adventure, and I must see the venture through. You wouldn't like me if I were a short sport. This doesn't mean, however, that I am sentencing myself for life; I am intending to resign just as soon as the opportunity comes. But really I ought to feel somewhat gratified that the Pendletons were willing to trust me with such a responsible post. Though you, my dear sir, do not suspect it, I possess considerable executive ability, and more common sense than is visible on the surface. If I chose to put my whole soul into this enterprise, I could make the rippingest surperintendent that any 111 orphans ever had.

I suppose you think that's funny? It's true. Judy and Jervis know it, and that's why they asked me to come. So you see, when they have shown so much confidence in me, I can't throw them over in quite the unceremonious fashion you suggest. So long as I am here, I am going to accomplish just as much as it is given one person to accomplish every twenty-four hours. I am going to turn the place over to my successor with things moving fast in the right direction.

But in the meantime please don't wash your hands of me under the belief that I'm too busy to be homesick; for I'm not. I wake up every morning and stare at Mrs. Lippett's wall-paper in a sort of daze, feeling as though it's some bad dream, and I'm not really here. What on earth was I thinking of to turn my back upon my nice cheerful own home and the good times that by rights are mine? I frequently agree with your opinion of my sanity.

But why, may I ask, should you be making such a fuss? You wouldn't be seeing me in any case. Worcester is quite as far from Washington as the John Grier Home. And I will add, for your further comfort, that whereas there is no man in the neighborhood of this asylum who admires red hair, in Worcester there are several. Therefore, most difficult of men, please be appeased. I didn't come entirely to spite you. I wanted an adventure in life, and, oh dear! oh dear! I'm having it!

Please write soon, and cheer me up.

Yours in sackcloth,
SALLIE.

Dear Judy:

You tell Jervis that I am not hasty at forming judgments. I have a sweet, sunny, unsuspicious nature, and I like everybody, almost. But no one could like that Scotch doctor. He *never* smiles.

He paid me another visit this afternoon. I invited him to accommodate himself in one of Mrs. Lippett's electric-blue chairs, and then sat down opposite to enjoy the harmony. He was dressed in a mustard-colored homespun, with a dash of green and a glint of yellow in the weave, a "heather mixture" calculated to add life to a dull Scotch moor. Purple socks and a red tie, with an amethyst pin, completed the picture. Clearly, your paragon of a doctor is not going to be of much assistance in pulling up the esthetic tone of this establishment.

During the fifteen minutes of his call he succinctly outlined all the changes he wishes to see accomplished in this institution. *He* forsooth! And what, may I ask, are the duties of a superintendent? Is she merely a figurehead to take orders from the visiting physician?

It's up wi' the bonnets o' McBride and MacRae!

I am,

Indignantly yours,
SALLIE.

THE JOHN GRIER HOME,
Monday.

Dear Dr. MacRae:

I am sending this note by Sadie Kate, as it seems impossible to reach you by telephone. Is the person who calls herself Mrs. McGur-rk and hangs up in the middle of a sentence your housekeeper? If she answers the telephone often, I don't see how your patients have any patience left.

As you did not come this morning, per agreement, and the painters did come, I was fain to choose a cheerful corn color to be placed upon the walls of your new laboratory room. I trust there is nothing unhygienic about corn color.

Also, if you can spare a moment this afternoon, kindly motor yourself to Dr. Brice's on Water Street and look at the dentist's chair and appurtenances which are to be had at half-price. If all of the pleasant paraphernalia of his profession were here,—in a corner of your laboratory,—Dr. Brice could finish his 111 new patients with much more despatch than if we had to transport them separately to Water Street. Don't you think that's a useful idea? It came to me in the middle of the night, but as I never happened to buy a dentist's chair before, I'd appreciate some professional advice.

Yours truly,
S. McBRIDE.

Dear Judy:

Do stop sending me telegrams!

Of course I know that you want to know everything that is happening, and I would send a daily bulletin, but I truly don't find a minute. I am so tired when night comes that if it weren't for Jane's strict discipline, I should go to bed with my clothes on.

Later, when we slip a little more into routine, and I can be sure that my assistants are all running off their respective jobs, I shall be the regularest correspondent you ever had.

It was five days ago, wasn't it, that I wrote? Things have been happening in those five days. The MacRae and I have mapped out a plan of campaign, and are stirring up this place to its sluggish depths. I like him less and less, but we have declared a sort of working truce. And the man *is* a worker. I always thought I had sufficient energy myself, but when an improvement is to be introduced, I toil along panting in his wake. He is as stubborn and tenacious and bulldoggish as a Scotchman can be, but he does understand babies; that is, he understands their physiological aspects. He hasn't any more feeling for them personally than for so many frogs that he might happen to be dissecting.

Do you remember Jervis's holding forth one evening for an hour or so about our doctor's beautiful humanitarian ideals? *C'est à rire!* The man merely regards the J. G. H. as his own private laboratory, where he can try out scientific

18

experiments with no loving parents to object. I shouldn't be surprised any day to find him introducing scarlet fever cultures into the babies' porridge in order to test a newly invented serum.

Of the house staff, the only two who strike me as really efficient are the primary teacher and the furnace-man. You should see how the children run to meet Miss Matthews and beg for caresses, and how painstakingly polite they are to the other teachers. Children are quick to size up character. I shall be very embarrassed if they are too polite to me.

Just as soon as I get my bearings a little, and know exactly what we need, I am going to accomplish some wide-spread discharging. I should like to begin with Miss Snaith; but I discover that she is the niece of one of our most generous trustees, and isn't exactly dischargeable. She's a vague, chinless, pale-eyed creature, who talks through her nose and breathes through her mouth. She can't say anything decisively and then stop; her sentences all trail off into incoherent murmurings. Every time I see the woman I feel an almost uncontrollable desire to take her by the shoulders and shake some decision into her. And Miss Snaith is the one who has had entire supervision of the seventeen little tots aged from two to five! But, anyway, even if I can't discharge her, I have reduced her to a subordinate position without her being aware of the fact.

The doctor has found for me a charming girl who lives a few miles from here and comes in every day to manage the kindergarten. She has big, gentle, brown eyes, like a cow's, and motherly manners (she is just nineteen), and the babies love her. At the head of the nursery I have placed a jolly, comfortable middle-aged woman who has

reared five of her own and has a hand with bairns. Our
doctor also found her; you see, he is useful. She is techni-
cally under Miss Snaith, but is usurping dictatorship in a
satisfactory fashion. I can now sleep at night without
being afraid that my babies are being inefficiently murdered.

You see, our reforms are getting started; and while I
acquiesce with all the intelligence at my command to our
doctor's basic scientific upheavals, still, they sometimes leave
me cold. The problem that keeps churning and churning
in my mind is, How can I ever instil enough love and
warmth and sunshine into those bleak little lives? And I
am not sure that the doctor's science will accomplish that.

One of our most pressing *intelligent* needs just now is to
get our records into coherent form. The books have been
most outrageously unkept. Mrs. Lippett had a big black
account-book into which she jumbled any facts that happened to drift her way as to the children's family, their
conduct, and their health; but for weeks at a time she didn't
trouble to make an entry. If any adopting family wants to
know a child's parentage, half the time we can't even tell
where we got the child!

> "Where did you come from, baby dear?"
> "The blue sky opened, and I am here,"

is an exact description of their arrival.

We need a field worker to travel about the country and
pick up all the hereditary statistics she can about our
chicks. It will be an easy matter, as most of them have
relatives. What do you think of Janet Ware for the job?
You remember what a shark she was in economics; she
simply battened on tables and charts and surveys.

I have also to inform you that the John Grier Home is undergoing a very searching physical examination, and it is the shocking truth that out of the twenty-eight poor little rats so far examined only five are up to specification. And the five have not been here long.

Do you remember the ugly green reception-room on the first floor? I have removed as much of its greenness as possible, and fitted it up as the doctor's laboratory. It contains scales and drugs and, most professional touch of all, a dentist's chair and one of those sweet grinding-machines. (Bought them second-hand from Doctor Brice in the village, who is putting in, for the gratification of his own patients, white enamel and nickel-plate.) That drilling-machine is looked upon as an infernal engine, and I as an infernal monster for instituting it. But every little victim who is discharged *filled* may come to my room every day for a week and receive two pieces of chocolate. Though our children are not conspicuously brave, they are, we discover, fighters. Young Thomas Kehoe nearly bit the doctor's thumb in two after kicking over a tableful of instruments. It requires physical strength as well as skill to be dental adviser to the J. G. H.

*   *   *

Interrupted here to show a benevolent lady over the institution. She asked fifty irrelevant questions, took up an hour of my time, then finally wiped away a tear and left a dollar for my "poor little charges."

So far, my poor little charges are not enthusiastic about these new reforms. They don't care much for the sudden draft of fresh air that has blown in upon them, or the deluge of water. I am shoving in two baths a week, and as

BATH MAT

SEVEN BATHS A WEEK!!

Unprecedented Cruelty on the part of an Orphan Asylum Superintendent

soon as we collect tubs enough and a few extra faucets, they are going to get *seven*.

But at least I have started one most popular reform. Our daily bill of fare has been increased, a change deplored by the cook as causing trouble, and deplored by the rest of the staff as causing an immoral increase in expense. ECON-OMY spelt in capitals has been the guiding principle of this institution for so many years that it has become a religion. I assure my timid co-workers twenty times a day that, owing to the generosity of our president, the endowment has been exactly doubled, and that I have vast sums besides from Mrs. Pendleton for necessary purposes like ice-cream. But they simply *can't* get over the feeling that it is a wicked extravagance to feed these children.

The doctor and I have been studying with care the menus of the past, and we are filled with amazement at the mind that could have devised them. Here is one of her frequently recurring dinners:

> Boiled potatoes
> Boiled rice
> Blanc mange

It's a wonder to me that the children are anything more than one hundred and eleven little lumps of starch.

Looking about this institution, one is moved to misquote Robert Browning.

> "There may be heaven; there must be hell;
> Meantime, there is the John Grier—well!"

S. McB.

Dear Judy:

Dr. Robin MacRae and I fought another battle yesterday over a very trivial matter (in which I was right), and since then I have adopted for our doctor a special pet name. "Good morning, Enemy!" was my greeting to-day, at which he was quite solemnly annoyed. He says he does not wish to be regarded as an enemy. He is not in the least antagonistic—so long as I mold my policy upon his wishes!

We have two new children, Isador Gutschneider and Max Yog, given to us by the Baptist Ladies' Aid Society. Where on earth do you suppose those children picked up such a religion? I didn't want to take them, but the poor ladies were very persuasive, and they pay the princely sum of four dollars and fifty cents per week per child. This

makes 113, which makes us very crowded. I have half a dozen babies to give away. Find me some kind families who want to adopt.

You know it's very embarrassing not to be able to remember offhand how large your family is, but mine seems to vary from day to day, like the stock market. I should like to keep it at about par. When a woman has more than a hundred children, she can't give them the individual attention they ought to have.

Monday.

This letter has been lying two days on my desk, and I haven't found the time to stick on a stamp. But now I seem to have a free evening ahead, so I will add a page or two more before starting it on a pleasant journey to Florida.

I am just beginning to pick out individual faces among the children; it seemed at first as though I could never learn them, they looked so hopelessly cut out of one pattern, with those unspeakably ugly uniforms. Now please don't write back that you want the children put into new clothes immediately. I know you do; you've already told me five times. In about a month I shall be ready to consider the question, but just now their insides are more important than their outsides.

There is no doubt about it—orphans in the mass do not appeal to me. I am beginning to be afraid that this famous mother instinct which we hear so much about was left out of my character. Children as children are dirty, spitty little things, and their noses all need wiping. Here and there I pick out a naughty, mischievous little one that awakens a flicker of interest; but for the most part they are just a composite blur of white face and blue check.

With one exception, though. Sadie Kate Kilcoyne emerged from the mass the first day, and bids fair to stay out for all time. She is my special little errand girl, and she furnishes me with all my daily amusement. No piece of mischief has been launched in this institution for the last eight years that did not originate in her abnormal brain. This young person has, to me, a most unusual history, though I understand it's common enough in foundling circles. She was discovered eleven years ago on the bottom step of a Thirty-ninth Street house, asleep in a pasteboard box labeled, "Altman & Co."

"Sadie Kate Kilcoyne, aged five weeks. Be kind to her," was neatly printed on the cover.

The policeman who picked her up took her to Bellevue, where the foundlings are pronounced, in the order of their arrival, "Catholic, Protestant, Catholic, Protestant," with perfect impartiality. Our Sadie Kate, despite her name and blue Irish eyes, was made a Protestant. And here she is growing Irisher and Irisher every day but, true to her christening, protesting loudly against every detail of life.

Her two little black braids point in opposite directions; her little monkey face is all screwed up with mischief; she is as active as a terrier, and you have to keep her busy every moment. Her record of badnesses occupies pages in the Doomsday Book. The last item reads:

"For stumping Maggie Geer to get a door-knob into her mouth—punishment, the afternoon spent in bed, and crackers for supper."

It seems that Maggie Geer, fitted with a mouth of unusual stretching capacity, got the door-knob in, but couldn't get it out. The doctor was called, and cannily solved the problem with a buttered shoe-horn. "Muckle-mouthed Meg," he has dubbed the patient ever since.

You can understand that my thoughts are anxiously occupied in filling every crevice of Sadie Kate's existence.

There are a million subjects that I ought to consult with the president about. I think it was very unkind of you and him to saddle me with your orphan-asylum and run off South to play. It would serve you right if I did everything wrong. While you are traveling about in private cars, and strolling in the moonlight on palm beaches, please think of me in the drizzle of a New York March, taking care of 113 babies that by rights are yours—and be grateful.

I remain (for a limited time),
S. McBride.

Dear Enemy:

I am sending herewith (under separate cover) Sammy Speir, who got mislaid when you paid your morning visit. Miss Snaith brought him to light after you had gone. Please scrutinize his thumb. I never saw a felon, but I have diagnosed it as such.

Yours truly,
S. McBRIDE.

SUP'T JOHN GRIER HOME,
March 6.

Dear Judy:

I don't know yet whether the children are going to love me or not, but they *do* love my dog. No creature so popular as Singapore ever entered these gates. Every afternoon three boys who have been perfect in deportment are allowed to brush and comb him, while three other good boys may serve him with food and drink. But every Saturday morning the climax of the week is reached, when three superlatively good boys give him a nice lathery bath with hot water and flea soap. The privilege of serving as Singapore's valet is going to be the only incentive I shall need for maintaining discipline.

But isn't it pathetically unnatural for these youngsters to be living in the country and never owning a pet? Especially when they, of all children, do so need something to love. I am going to manage pets for them somehow, if I have to spend our new endowment for a menagerie. Couldn't you bring back some baby alligators and a pelican? Anything alive will be gratefully received.

This should by rights be my first "Trustees' Day." I am deeply grateful to Jervis for arranging a simple business meeting in New York, as we are not yet on dress parade up here; but we are hoping by the first Wednesday in April to have something visible to show. If all of the doctor's ideas, and a few of my own, get themselves materialized, our trustees will open their eyes a bit when we show them about.

I have just made out a chart for next week's meals, and

29

posted it in the kitchen in the sight of an aggrieved cook. Variety is a word hitherto not found in the lexicon of the J. G. H. You would never dream all of the delightful surprises we are going to have: brown bread, corn pone, graham muffins, samp, rice pudding with *lots* of raisins, thick vegetable soup, macaroni Italian fashion, polenta cakes with molasses, apple-dumplings, ginger-bread—oh, an endless list! After our biggest girls have assisted in the manufacture of such appetizing dainties, they will almost be capable of keeping future husbands in love with them.

Oh, dear me! Here I am babbling these silly nothings when I have some real news up my sleeve. We have a new worker, a gem of a worker.

Do you remember Betsy Kindred, 1910? She led the glee club and was president of dramatics. I remember her perfectly; she always had lovely clothes. Well, if you please, she lives only twelve miles from here. I ran across her by chance yesterday morning as she was motoring through the village; or, rather, she just escaped running across me.

I never spoke to her in my life, but we greeted each other like the oldest friends. It pays to have conspicuous hair; she recognized me instantly. I hopped upon the running-board of her car and said:

"Betsy Kindred, 1910, you've got to come back to my orphan-asylum and help me catalogue my orphans."

And it astonished her so that she came. She's to be here four or five days a week as temporary secretary, and somehow I must manage to keep her permanently. She's the most useful person I ever saw. I am hoping that orphans will become such a habit with her that she won't be able to give them up. I think she might stay if we pay her a big enough salary. She likes to be independent of her family, as do all of us in these degenerate times.

In my growing zeal for cataloguing people, I should like to get our doctor tabulated. If Jervis knows any gossip about him, write it to me, please; the worse, the better. He called yesterday to lance a felon on Sammy Speir's thumb, then ascended to my electric-blue parlor to give instructions as to the dressing of thumbs. The duties of a superintendent are manifold.

It was just tea-time, so I casually asked him to stay, and he did! Not for the pleasure of my society,—no, indeed, —but because Jane appeared at the moment with a plate of toasted muffins. He hadn't had any luncheon, it seems, and dinner was a long way ahead. Between muffins (he ate the whole plateful) he saw fit to interrogate me as to my preparedness for this position. Had I studied biology in college? How far had I gone in chemistry? What did I know of sociology? Had I visited that model institution at Hastings?

To all of which I responded affably and openly. Then I permitted myself a question or two: just what sort of youthful training had been required to produce such a model of logic, accuracy, dignity, and common sense as I saw sitting before me? Through persistent prodding I elicited a few forlorn facts, but all quite respectable. You'd think, from his reticence, there'd been a hanging in the family. The MacRae *père* was born in Scotland, and came to the States to occupy a chair at Johns Hopkins; son Robin was shipped back to Auld Reekie for his education. His grandmother was a M'Lachlan of Strathlachan (I am sure she sounds respectable), and his vacations were spent in the Hielands a-chasing the deer.

So much could I gather; so much, and no more. Tell me, I beg, some gossip about my enemy—something scandalous by preference.

Why, if he is such an awfully efficient person does he bury himself in this remote locality? You would think an up-and-coming scientific man would want a hospital at one elbow and a morgue at the other. Are you sure that he didn't commit a crime and isn't hiding from the law?

I seem to have covered a lot of paper without telling you much. *Vive la bagatelle!*

Yours as usual,
SALLIE.

P.S. I am relieved on one point. Dr. MacRae does not pick out his own clothes. He leaves all such unessential trifles to his housekeeper, Mrs. Maggie McGurk.

Again, and irrevocably, good-by!

THE JOHN GRIER HOME,
Wednesday.

Dear Gordon:
Your roses and your letter cheered me for an entire
morning, and it's the first time I've approached cheerfulness since the fourteenth of February, when I waved
good-by to Worcester.

Words can't tell you how monotonously oppressive the
daily round of institution life gets to be. The only glimmer
in the whole dull affair is the fact that Betsy Kindred
spends four days a week with us. Betsy and I were in
college together, and we do occasionally find something
funny to laugh about.

Yesterday we were having tea in my *hideous* parlor when
we suddenly determined to revolt against so much unnecessary ugliness. We called in six sturdy and destructive
orphans, a step-ladder, and a bucket of hot water, and in
two hours had every vestige of that tapestry paper off those
walls. You can't imagine what fun it is ripping paper off
walls.

Two paper-hangers are at work this moment hanging
the best that our village affords, while a German uphol-
sterer is on his knees measuring my chairs for chintz
slip-covers that will hide every inch of their plush
upholstery.

Please don't get nervous. This doesn't mean that I'm
preparing to spend my life in the asylum. It means only
that I'm preparing a cheerful welcome for my successor. I
haven't dared tell Judy how dismal I find it, because I
don't want to cloud Florida; but when she returns to New

33

York she will find my official resignation waiting to meet her in the front hall.

I would write you a long letter in grateful payment for seven pages, but two of my little dears are holding a fight under the window. I dash to separate them.

Yours as ever,
S. McB.

My *dear* Judy:

I myself have bestowed a little present upon the John Grier Home—the refurnishing of the superintendent's private parlor. I saw the first night here that neither I nor any future occupant could be happy with Mrs. Lippett's electric plush. You see, I am planning to make my successor contented and willing to stay.

Betsy Kindred assisted in the rehabilitation of the Lippett's chamber of horrors, and between us we have created a symphony in dull blue and gold. Really and truly, it's one of the loveliest rooms you've ever seen; the sight of it will be an artistic education to any orphan. New paper on the wall, new rugs on the floor (my own prized Persians expressed from Worcester by an expostulating family). New casement curtains at my three windows, revealing a wide and charming view, hitherto hidden by Nottingham lace. A new big table, some lamps and books and a picture or so, and a real open fire. She had closed the fireplace because it let in air.

I never realized what a difference artistic surroundings make in the peace of one's soul. I sat last night and watched my fire throw nice high lights on my new old fender, and purred with contentment. And I assure you it's the first purr that has come from this cat since she entered the gates of the John Grier Home.

But the refurnishing of the superintendent's parlor is the slightest of our needs. The children's private apartments demand so much basic attention that I can't decide where to begin. That dark north playroom is a shocking scandal, but no more shocking than our hideous dining-room or our unventilated dormitories or our tubless lavatories.

If the institution is very saving, do you think it can ever afford to burn down this smelly old original building, and put up instead some nice, ventilated modern cottages? I cannot contemplate that wonderful institution at Hastings without being filled with envy. It would be some fun to run an asylum if you had a plant like that to work with. But, anyway, when you get back to New York and are ready to consult the architect about remodeling, please apply to me for suggestions. Among other little details I want two hundred feet of sleeping-porch running along the outside of our dormitories.

You see, it's this way: our physical examination reveals the fact that about half of our children are ænemic— aneamic—anæmic (Mercy! what a word!), and a lot of them have tubercular ancestors, and more have alcoholic. Their first need is oxygen rather than education. And if the sickly ones need it, why wouldn't it be good for the well ones? I should like to have every child, winter and summer, sleeping in the open air; but I know that if I let fall such a bomb on the board of trustees, the whole body would explode.

Speaking of trustees, I have met up with the Hon. Cyrus Wykoff, and I really believe that I dislike him more than Dr. Robin MacRae or the kindergarten teacher or the cook. I seem to have a genius for discovering enemies!

Mr. Wykoff called on Wednesday last to look over the new superintendent.

Having lowered himself into my most comfortable arm-chair, he proceeded to spend the day. He asked my fa-

ther's business, and whether or not he was well-to-do. I
told him that my father manufactured overalls, and that,
even in these hard times, the demand for overalls was
pretty steady.

He seemed relieved; he approves of the utilitarian as-
pect of overalls. He had been afraid that I had come from
the family of a minister or professor or writer, a lot of high
thinking and no common sense. Cyrus believes in common
sense.

And what had been my training for this position?

That, as you know, is a slightly embarrassing question.
But I produced my college education and a few lectures
at the School of Philanthropy, also a short residence
in the college settlement (I didn't tell him that all I
had done there was to paint the back hall and stairs).
Then I submitted some social work among my father's
employees and a few friendly visits to the Home for Female
Inebriates.

To all of which he grunted.

I added that I had lately made a study of the care of
dependent children, and casually mentioned my seventeen
institutions.

He grunted again, and said he didn't take much stock
in this new-fangled scientific charity.

At this point Jane entered with a box of roses from
the florist's. That blessed Gordon Hallock sends me
roses twice a week to brighten the rigors of institution
life.

Our trustee began an indignant investigation. He wished
to know where I got those flowers, and was visibly relieved
when he learned that I had not spent the institution's
money for them. He next wished to know who Jane might

be. I had foreseen that question and decided to brazen it out.

"My maid," said I.

"Your what?" he bellowed, quite red in the face.

"My maid."

"What is she doing here?"

I amiably went into details. "She mends my clothes, blacks my boots, keeps my bureau drawers in order, washes my hair."

I really thought the man would choke, so I charitably added that I paid her wages out of my own private income, and paid five dollars and fifty cents a week to the institution for her board; and that, though she was big, she didn't eat much.

He allowed that I might make use of one of the orphans for all legitimate service.

I explained—still polite, but growing bored—that Jane had been in my service for many years, and was indispensable.

He finally took himself off, after telling me that he, for one, had never found any fault with Mrs. Lippett. She was a common-sense Christian woman, without many fancy ideas, but with plenty of good solid work in her. He hoped that I would be wise enough to model my policy upon hers!

And what, my dear Judy, do you think of that?

The doctor dropped in a few minutes later, and I repeated the Hon. Cyrus's conversation in detail. For the first time in the history of our intercourse the doctor and I agreed.

"Mrs. Lippett indeed!" he growled. "The blethering auld gomerel! May the Lord send him mair sense!"

When our doctor really becomes aroused, he drops into

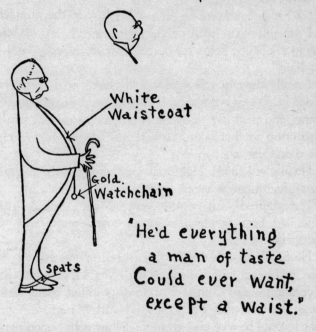

The Honorable Cyrus Wykoff

White Waistcoat

Gold Watchchain

spats

"He'd everything
a man of taste
Could ever want,
except a waist."

Scotch. My latest pet name for him (behind his back) is
Sandy.

Sadie Kate is sitting on the floor as I write, untangling
sewing-silks and winding them neatly for Jane, who is
becoming quite attached to the little imp.

"I am writing to your Aunt Judy," say I to Sadie Kate.
"What message shall I send from you?"

"I never heard of no Aunt Judy."

"She is the aunt of every good little girl in this school."

"Tell her to come and visit me and bring some candy,"
says Sadie Kate.

I say so, too.

My love to the president,
SALLIE.

MRS. JUDY ABBOTT PENDLETON,

Dear Madam:

Your four letters, two telegrams, and three checks are at
hand, and your instructions shall be obeyed just as quickly
as this overworked superintendent can manage it.

I delegated the dining-room job to Betsy Kindred. One
hundred dollars did I allow her for the rehabilitation of
that dreary apartment. She accepted the trust, picked out
five likely orphans to assist in the mechanical details, and
closed the door. For three days the children have been
eating from the desks in the schoolroom. I haven't an
idea what Betsy is doing; but she has a lot better taste
than I, so there isn't much use in interfering.

It is such a heaven-sent relief to be able to leave
something to somebody else, and be sure it will be carried
out! With all due respect to the age and experience of the
staff I found here, they are not very open to new ideas. As
the John Grier Home was planned by its noble founder in
1875, so shall it be run to-day.

Incidentally, my dear Judy, your idea of a private dining-
room for the superintendent, which I, being a social soul,
at first scorned, has been my salvation. When I am dead
tired I dine alone, but in my live intervals I invite an
officer to share the meal; and in the expansive intimacy of
the dinner-table I get in my most effective strokes. When
it becomes desirable to plant the seeds of fresh air in the
soul of Miss Snaith, I invite her to dinner, and tactfully
sandwich in a little oxygen between her slices of pressed
veal.

Pressed veal is our cook's idea of an acceptable *pièce de résistance* or a dinner party. In another month I am going to face the subject of suitable nourishment for the executive staff; meanwhile there are so many things more important than our own comfort that we shall have to worry along on veal.

A terrible bumping has just occurred outside my door. One little cherub seems to be kicking another little cherub downstairs. But I write on undisturbed. If I am to spend my days among orphans, I must cultivate a cheerful detachment.

Did you get Leonora Fenton's cards? She's marrying a medical missionary and going to Siam to live! Did you ever hear of anything so absurd as Leonora presiding over a missionary's *ménage*? Do you suppose she will entertain the heathen with skirt dances?

It isn't any absurder, though, than me in an orphan-asylum, or you as a conservative settled matron, or Marty Keene a social butterfly in Paris. Do you suppose she goes to embassy balls in riding-clothes, and what on earth does she do about hair? It couldn't have grown so soon; she must wear a wig. Isn't our class turning out some hilarious surprises?

The mail arrives. Excuse me while I read a nice fat letter from Washington.

Not so nice; quite impertinent. Gordon can't get over the idea that it is a joke, S. McB. in conjunction with one hundred and thirteen orphans. But he wouldn't think it such a joke if he could try it for a few days. He says he is going to drop off here on his next trip North and watch the struggle. How would it be if I left him in charge while

I dashed to New York to accomplish some shopping? Our sheets are all worn out, and we haven't more than two hundred and eleven blankets in the house.

Singapore, sole puppy of my heart and home, sends his respectful love.

I also,
S. McB.

THE JOHN GRIER HOME,
Friday.

My dearest Judy:

You should see what your hundred dollars and Betsy Kindred did to that dining-room!

It's a dazzling dream of yellow paint. Being a north room, she thought to brighten it; and she has. The walls are kalsomined buff, with a frieze of little molly cotton-tails scurrying around the top. All of the woodwork—tables and benches included—is a cheerful chrome yellow. Instead of table-cloths, which we can't afford, we have linen runners, with stenciled rabbits hopping along their length. Also yellow bowls, filled at present with pussy-willows, but looking forward to dandelions and cowslips and buttercups. And new dishes, my dear—white, with yellow jonquils (we think), though they may be roses; there is no botany expert in the house. Most wonderful touch of all, we have *napkins*, the first we have seen in our whole lives. The children thought they were handkerchiefs, and ecstatically wiped their noses.

To honor the opening of the new room, we had ice-cream and cake for dessert. It is such a pleasure to see these children anything but cowed and apathetic, that I am offering prizes for boisterousness—to every one but Sadie Kate. She drummed on the table with her knife and fork and sang, "Welcome to dem golden halls."

You remember that illuminated text over the dining-room door—"The Lord Will Provide." We've painted it

44

Betsy and five
husky Orphans decorate
the dining-room

out, and covered the spot with rabbits. It's all very well to teach so easy a belief to normal children, who have a proper family and roof behind them; but a person whose only refuge in distress will be a park bench must learn a more militant creed than that.

"The Lord has given you two hands and a brain and a big world to use them in. Use them well, and you will be provided for; use them ill, and you will want," is our motto, and that with reservations.

In the sorting process that has been going on I have got rid of eleven children. That blessed State Charities Aid Association helped me dispose of three little girls, all placed in very nice homes, and one to be adopted legally if the family likes her. And the family will like her; I saw to that. She was the prize child of the institution, obedient and polite, with curly hair and affectionate ways, exactly the little girl that every family needs. When a couple of adopting parents are choosing a daughter, I stand by with my heart in my mouth, feeling as though I were assisting in the inscrutable designs of Fate. Such a little thing turns the balance! The child smiles, and a loving home is hers for life; she sneezes, and it passes her by forever.

Three of our biggest boys have gone to work on farms, one of them out West to a RANCH! Report has it that he is to become a cow-boy and Indian fighter and grizzly-bear hunter, though I believe in reality he is to engage in the pastoral work of harvesting wheat. He marched off, a hero of romance, followed by the wistful eyes of twenty-five adventurous lads, who turned back with a sigh to the safely monotonous life of the J. G. H.

Five other children have been sent to their proper institutions. One of them is deaf, one an epileptic, and the other three approaching idiocy. None of them ought ever to have been accepted here. This is an educational institution, and we can't waste our valuable plant in caring for defectives.

Orphan-asylums have gone out of style. What I am going to develop is a boarding-school for the physical, moral, and mental growth of children whose parents have not been able to provide for their care.

"Orphans" is merely my generic term for the children; a good many of them are not orphans in the least. They have one troublesome and tenacious parent left who won't sign a surrender, so I can't place them out for adoption. But those that are available would be far better off in loving foster-homes than in the best institution that I can ever make. So I am fitting them for adoption as quickly as possible, and searching for the homes.

You ought to run across a lot of pleasant families in your travels; can't you bully some of them into adopting children? Boys by preference. We've got an awful lot of extra boys, and nobody wants them. Talk about anti-feminism! It's nothing to the anti-masculism that exists in the breasts of adopting parents. I could place out a thousand dimpled little girls with yellow hair, but a good live boy from nine to thirteen is a drug on the market. There seems to be a general feeling that they track in dirt and scratch up mahogany furniture.

Shouldn't you think that men's clubs might like to adopt boys, as a sort of mascot? The boy could be boarded in a nice respectable family, and drawn out by

the different members on Saturday afternoons. They
could take him to ball-games and the circus, and then
return him when they had had enough, just as you do with
a library book. It would be very valuable training for
the bachelors. People are forever talking about the
desirability of training girls for motherhood. Why not
institute a course of training in fatherhood, and get the
best men's clubs to take it up? Will you please have

Jervis agitate the matter at his various clubs, and I'll have Gordon start the idea in Washington. They both belong to such a lot of clubs that we ought to dispose of at least a dozen boys.

I remain,

The ever-distracted mother of 113.

S. McB.

Dear Judy:

I have been having a pleasant respite from the 113 cares of motherhood.

Yesterday who should drop down upon our peaceful village but Mr. Gordon Hallock, on his way back to Washington to resume the cares of the nation. At least he said it was on his way, but I notice from the map in the primary room that it was one hundred miles out of his way.

And dear, but I was glad to see him! He is the first glimpse of the outside world I have had since I was incarcerated in this asylum. And such a lot of entertaining businesses he had to talk about! He knows the inside of all of the outside things you read in the newspapers; so far as I can make out, he is the social center about which Washington revolves. I always knew he would get on in politics, for he has a way with him; there's no doubt about it.

You can't imagine how exhilarated and set-up I feel, as though I'd come into my own again after a period of social ostracism. I must confess that I get lonely for some one who talks my kind of nonsensical talk. Betsy trots off home every week-end, and the doctor is conversational enough, but, oh, so horribly logical! Gordon somehow seems to stand for the life I belong to,—of country clubs and motors and dancing and sport and politeness,—a poor, foolish, silly life, if you will, but mine own. And I have missed it. This serving-society business is theoretically admirable and compelling and interesting, but deadly stupid in its working details. I am afraid I was never born to set the crooked straight.

I tried to show Gordon about and make him take an interest in the babies, but he wouldn't glance at them. He thinks I came just to spite him, which, of course, I did. Your siren call would never have lured me from the path of frivolity had Gordon not been so unpleasantly hilarious at the idea of my being able to manage an orphan-asylum. I came here to show him that I could; and now, when I *can* show him, the beast refuses to look.

I invited him to dinner, with a warning about the pressed veal; but he said no, thanks, that I needed a change. So we went to Brantwood Inn and had broiled lobster. I had positively forgotten that the creatures were edible.

This morning at seven o'clock I was wakened by the furious ringing of the telephone bell. It was Gordon at the station, about to resume his journey to Washington. He was in quite a contrite mood about the asylum, and apologized largely for refusing to look at my children. It was not that he didn't like orphans, he said; it was just that he didn't like them in juxtaposition to me. And to prove his good intentions, he would send them a bag of peanuts.

I feel as fresh and revivified after my little fling as though I'd had a real vacation. There's no doubt about it, an hour or so of exciting talk is more of a tonic to me than a pint of iron and strychnine pills.

You owe me two letters, dear Madam. Pay them *tout de suite,* or I lay down my pen forever.

Yours, as usual,
S. McB.

My *dear* Enemy:

I am told that during my absence this afternoon you paid us a call and dug up a scandal. You claim that the children under Miss Snaith are not receiving their due in the matter of cod-liver oil.

I am sorry if your medicinal orders have not been carried out, but you must know that it is a difficult matter to introduce that abominably smelling stuff into the inside of a squirming child. And poor Miss Snaith is a very much overworked person. She has ten more children to care for than should rightly fall to the lot of any single woman, and until we find her another assistant, she has very little time for the fancy touches you demand.

Also, my dear Enemy, she is very susceptible to abuse. When you feel in a fighting mood, I wish you would expend your belligerence upon me. I don't mind it; quite the contrary. But that poor lady has retired to her room in a state of hysterics, leaving nine babies to be tucked into bed by whomever it may concern.

If you have any powders that would be settling to her nerves, please send them back by Sadie Kate.

Yours truly,
S. McBRIDE.

Wednesday morning.

Dear Dr. MacRae:

I am not taking an unintelligent stand in the least; I am simply asking that you come to me with all complaints, and not stir up my staff in any such volcanic fashion as that of yesterday.

I endeavor to carry out all of your orders—of a medical nature—with scrupulous care. In the present case there seems to have been some negligence; I don't know what did become of those fourteen unadministered bottles of cod-liver oil that you have made such a fuss about, but I shall investigate.

And I cannot, for various reasons, pack off Miss Snaith in the summary fashion you demand. She may be, in certain respects, inefficient; but she is kind to the children, and with supervision will answer temporarily.

Yours truly,
S. MCBRIDE.

Thursday.

Dear Enemy:

Soyez tranquille. I have issued orders, and in the future the children shall receive all of the cod-liver oil that by rights is theirs. A wilfu' man maun' hae his way.

S. McB.

March 22.

Dear Judy:

Asylum life has looked up a trifle during the past few days—since the great Cod-Liver Oil War has been raging. The first skirmish occurred on Tuesday, and I unfortunately missed it, having accompanied four of my children on a shopping trip to the village. I returned to find the asylum teeming with hysterics. Our explosive doctor had paid us a visit.

Sandy has two passions in life: one is for cod-liver oil and the other for spinach, neither popular in our nursery. Some time ago—before I came, in fact—he had ordered cod-liver oil for all of the
$\begin{Bmatrix} \text{ænemic} \\ \text{aneamic} \end{Bmatrix}$ —Heavens! there's that word again!—
children, and had given instructions as to its application to Miss Snaith. Yesterday in his suspicious Scotch fashion, he began nosing about to find out why the poor little rats weren't fattening up as fast as he thought they ought, and he unearthed a hideous scandal. They haven't received a whiff of cod-liver oil for three whole weeks! At that point he exploded, and all was joy and excitement and hysterics.

Betsy says that she had to send Sadie Kate to the laundry on an improvised errand, as his language was not fit for orphan ears. By the time I got home he had gone, and Miss Snaith had retired, weeping, to her room, and the whereabouts of fourteen bottles of cod-liver oil was still unexplained. He had accused her at the top of his voice of taking them herself. Imagine Miss Snaith,—she who looks so innocent and chinless and inoffensive—stealing

55

cod-liver oil from these poor helpless little orphans and guzzling it in private!

Her defense consisted in hysterical assertions that she loved the children, and had done her duty as she saw it. She did not believe in giving medicine to babies; she thought drugs bad for their poor little stomachs. You can imagine Sandy! Oh, dear! oh, dear! To think I missed it!

Well, the tempest raged for three days, and Sadie Kate nearly ran her little legs off carrying peppery messages back and forth between us and the doctor. It is only under stress that I communicate with him by telephone, as he has an interfering old termagant of a housekeeper who "listens in" on the down-stairs switch; I don't wish the scandalous secrets of the John Grier spread abroad. The doctor demanded Miss Snaith's instant dismissal, and I refused. Of course she is a vague, unfocused, inefficient old thing, but she does love the children, and with proper supervision is fairly useful.

At least, in the light of her exalted family connections, I can't pack her off in disgrace like a drunken cook. I am hoping in time to eliminate her by a process of delicate suggestion; perhaps I can make her feel that her health requires a winter in California. And also, no matter what the doctor wants, so positive and dictatorial is his manner that just out of self-respect one must take the other side. When he states that the world is round, I instantly assert it to be triangular.

Finally, after three pleasantly exhilarating days, the whole business settled itself. An apology (a very dilute one) was extracted from him for being so unkind to the poor lady, and full confession, with promises for the future, was drawn from her. It seems that she couldn't bear to make the little dears take the stuff, but, for obvious reasons, she couldn't bear to cross Dr. MacRae, so she hid the last fourteen bottles in a dark corner of the cellar. Just how she was planning to dispose of her loot I don't know. Can you pawn cod-liver oil?

LATER.

Peace negotiations had just ended this afternoon, and Sandy had made a dignified exit, when the Hon. Cyrus Wykoff was announced. Two enemies in the course of an hour are really too much!

The Hon. Cy was awfully impressed with the new dining-room, especially when he heard that Betsy had put on those rabbits with her own lily-white hands. Stenciling rabbits on walls, he allows, is a fitting pursuit for a woman, but an executive position like mine is a trifle out of her sphere. He thinks it would be far wiser if Mr. Pendleton did not give me such free scope in the spending of his money.

While we were still contemplating Betsy's mural flight, an awful crash came from the pantry, and we found Gladiola Murphy weeping among the ruins of five yellow plates. It is sufficiently shattering to my nerves to hear these crashes when I am alone, but it is peculiarly shattering when receiving a call from an unsympathetic trustee.

I shall cherish that set of dishes to the best of my ability, but if you wish to see your gift in all its uncracked beauty, I should advise you to hurry North, and visit the John Grier Home without delay.

Yours as ever,
SALLIE.

My dear Judy:

I have just been holding an interview with a woman who wants to take a baby home to surprise her husband. I had a hard time convincing her that, since he is to support the child, it might be a delicate attention to consult him about its adoption. She argued stubbornly that it was none of his business, seeing that the onerous work of washing and dressing and training would fall upon her. I am really beginning to feel sorry for men. Some of them seem to have very few rights.

Even our pugnacious doctor I suspect of being a victim of domestic tyranny, and his housekeeper's at that. It is scandalous the way Maggie McGurk neglects the poor man. I have had to put him in charge of an orphan. Sadie Kate, with a very housewifely air, is this moment sitting cross-legged on the hearth rug sewing buttons on his overcoat while he is upstairs tending babies.

You would never believe it, but Sandy and I are growing quite confidential in a dour Scotch fashion. It has become his habit, when homeward bound after his professional calls, to chug up to our door about four in the afternoon, and make the rounds of the house to make sure that we are not developing cholera morbus or infanticide or anything catching, and then present himself at four-thirty at my library door to talk over our mutual problems.

Does he come to see me? Oh, no, indeed; he comes to get tea and toast and marmalade. The man hath a lean and hungry look. His housekeeper doesn't feed him enough.

As soon as I get the upper hand of him a little more, I am going to urge him on to revolt.

Meanwhile he is very grateful for something to eat, but oh, so funny in his attempts at social grace! At first he would hold a cup of tea in one hand, a plate of muffins in the other, and then search blankly for a third hand to eat them with. Now he has solved the problem. He turns in his toes and brings his knees together; then he folds his napkin into a long, narrow wedge that fills the crack between them, thus forming a very workable pseudo-lap; after that he sits with tense muscles until the tea is drunk. I suppose I ought to provide a table, but the spectacle of Sandy with his toes turned in is the one gleam of amusement that my day affords.

The postman is just driving in with, I trust, a letter from you. Letters make a very interesting break in the monotony of asylum life. If you wish to keep this superintendent contented, you'd better write often.

*   *   *

Mail received and contents noted.

Kindly convey my thanks to Jervis for three alligators in a swamp. He shows rare artistic taste in the selection of his post-cards. Your seven-page illustrated letter from Miami arrives at the same time. I should have known Jervis from the palm-tree perfectly, even without the label, as the tree has so much the more hair of the two. Also, I have a polite bread-and-butter letter from my nice young man in Washington, and a book from him, likewise a box of candy. The bag of peanuts for the kiddies he has shipped by express. Did you ever know such assiduity?

Jimmie favors me with the news that he is coming to visit me as soon as father can spare him from the factory. The poor boy does hate that factory so! It isn't that he is lazy; he just simply isn't interested in overalls. But father can't understand such a lack of taste. Having built up the factory, he of course has developed a passion for overalls, which should have been inherited by his eldest son. I find it awfully convenient to have been born a daughter; I am not asked to like overalls, but am left free to follow any morbid career I may choose, such as this.

To return to my mail: There arrives an advertisement from a wholesale grocer, saying that he has exceptionally economical brands of oatmeal, rice, flour, prunes, and dried apples that he packs specially for prisons and charitable institutions. Sounds nutritious, doesn't it?

I also have letters from a couple of farmers, each of whom would like to have a strong, husky boy of fourteen who is not afraid of work, their object being to give him a good home. These good homes appear with great frequency just as the spring planting is coming on. When we investigated one of them last week, the village minister, in answer to our usual question, "Does he own any property?" replied in a very guarded manner, "I think he must own a corkscrew."

You would hardly credit some of the homes that we have investigated. We found a very prosperous country family the other day, who lived huddled together in three rooms in order to keep the rest of their handsome house clean. The fourteen-year girl they wished to adopt, by way of a cheap servant, was to sleep in the same tiny room with their own three children. Their kitchen-dining-parlor apartment was more cluttered up and unaired than any city tenement I ever saw, and the thermometer at eighty-four.

One could scarcely say they were *living* there; they were rather *cooking*. You may be sure they got no girl from us!

I have made one invariable rule—every other is flexible. No child is to be placed out unless the proposed family can offer better advantages than we can give. I mean than we are going to be able to give in the course of a few months, when we get ourselves made over into a model institution. I shall have to confess that at present we are still pretty bad.

But anyway, I am very *choosey* in regard to homes, and I reject three-fourths of those that offer.

LATER.

Gordon has made honorable amends to my children. His bag of peanuts is here, made of burlap and three feet high.

Do you remember the dessert of peanuts and maple
sugar they used to give us at college? We turned up our
noses, but ate. I am instituting it here, and I assure you we
don't turn up our noses. It is a pleasure to feed children
who have graduated from a course of Mrs. Lippett; they
are pathetically grateful for small blessings.

You can't complain that this letter is too short.

                              Yours,
                    On the verge of writer's cramp,
                                        S. McB.

Dear Judy:

You will be interested to hear that I have encountered
another enemy—the doctor's housekeeper. I had talked to
the creature several times over the telephone, and had
noted that her voice was not distinguished by the soft, low
accents that mark the caste of "Vere de Vere"; but now I
have seen her. This morning, while returning from the
village, I made a slight detour, and passed our doctor's
house. Sandy is evidently the result of environment—olive
green, with a mansard roof and the shades pulled down.
You would think he had just been holding a funeral. I
don't wonder that the amenities of life have somewhat
escaped the poor man. After studying the outside of his
house, I was filled with curiosity to see if the inside
matched.

Having sneezed five times before breakfast this morning, I decided to go in and consult him professionally. To
be sure, he is a children's specialist, but sneezes are common to all ages. So I boldly marched up the steps and rang
the bell.

Hark! What sound is that that breaks upon our revelry?
The Hon. Cy's voice, as I live, approaching up the
stairs. I've letters to write, and I can't be tormented
by his blether, so I am rushing Jane to the door with
orders to look him firmly in the eye and tell him I
am out.

* * * * * * * *

On with the dance! Let joy be unconfined. He's gone.

But those eight stars represent eight agonizing minutes spent in the dark of my library closet. The Hon. Cy received Jane's communication with the affable statement that he would sit down and wait. Whereupon he entered and sat. But did Jane leave me to languish in the closet? No; she enticed him to the nursery to see the *awful* thing that Sadie Kate has done. The Hon. Cy loves to see awful things, particularly when done by Sadie Kate. I haven't an idea what scandal Jane is about to disclose; but no matter, he has gone.

Where was I? Oh, yes; I had rung the doctor's bell.

The door was opened by a large, husky person with her sleeves rolled up. She looked very businesslike, with a hawk's nose and cold gray eyes.

"Well?" said she, her tone implying that I was a vacuum-cleaning agent.

"Good morning." I smiled affably, and stepped inside. "Is this Mrs. McGurk?"

"It is," said she. "An' ye'll be the new young woman in the orphan-asylum?"

"I am that," said I. "Is himself at home?"

"He is not," said she.

"But this is his office hour."

"He don't keep it regular'."

"He ought," said I, sternly. "Kindly tell him that Miss McBride called to consult him, and ask him to look in at the John Grier Home this afternoon."

"Ump'!" grunted Mrs. McGurk, and closed the door so promptly that she shut in the hem of my skirt.

When I told the doctor this afternoon, he shrugged his shoulders, and observed that that was Maggie's gracious way.

"And why do you put up with Maggie?" said I.

"And where would I find any one better?" said he. "Doing the work for a lone man who comes as irregularly to meals as a twenty-four-hour day will permit is no sinecure. She furnishes little sunshine in the home, but she does manage to produce a hot dinner at nine o'clock at night."

Just the same, I am willing to wager that her hot dinners are neither delicious nor well served. She's an inefficent, lazy old termagant, and I know why she doesn't like me. She imagines that I want to steal away the doctor and oust her from a comfortable position, something of a joke, considering. But I am not undeceiving her; it will do the old thing good to worry a little. She may cook him better dinners, and fatten him up a trifle. I understand that fat men are good-natured.

Ten o'clock.

I don't know what silly stuff I have been writing to you off and on all day, between interruptions. It has got to be night at last, and I am too tired to do so much as hold up my head. Your song tells the sad truth, "There is no joy in life but sleep."

I bid you good night.

S. McB.

Isn't the English language absurd? Look at those forty monosyllables in a row!

Dear Judy:

I have placed out Isador Gutschneider. His new mother is a Swedish woman, fat and smiling, with blue eyes and yellow hair. She chose him out of the whole nurseryful of children because he was the brunettest baby there. She has always loved brunettes, but in her most ambitious dreams has never hoped to have one of her own. His name is going to be changed to Oscar Carlson, after his new dead uncle.

My first trustees' meeting is to occur next Wednesday. I confess that I am not looking forward to it with impatience—especially as an inaugural address by me will be its chief feature. I wish our president were here to back me up! But at least I am sure of one thing. I am never going to adopt the Uriah Heepish attitude toward trustees that characterized Mrs. Lippett's manners. I shall treat "first Wednesdays" as a pleasant social diversion, my day at home, when the friends of the asylum gather for discussion and relaxation; and I shall endeavor not to let our pleasures discommode the orphans. You see how I have taken to heart the unhappy experiences of that little Jerusha.

Your last letter has arrived, and no suggestion in it of traveling North. Isn't it about time that you were turning your faces back toward Fifth Avenue? Hame is hame, be't ever sae hamely. Don't you marvel at the Scotch that flows so readily from my pen? Since being acquent' wi' Sandy, I hae gathered a muckle new vocabulary.

The dinner gong! I leave you, to devote a revivifying half-hour to mutton hash. We eat to live in the John Grier Home.

SIX O'CLOCK.

The Hon. Cy has been calling again; he drops in with great frequency, hoping to catch me *in delictu.* How I do not like that man! He is a pink, fat, puffy old thing, with a pink, fat, puffy soul. I was in a very cheery, optimistic frame of mind before his arrival, but now I shall do nothing but grumble for the rest of the day.

He deplores all of the useless innovations that I am endeavoring to introduce, such as a cheerful playroom, prettier clothes, baths, and better food and fresh air and play and fun and ice-cream and kisses. He says that I will unfit these children to occupy the position in life that God has called them to occupy.

At that my Irish blood came to the surface, and I told him that if God had planned to make all of these 113 little children into useless, ignorant, unhappy citizens, I was going to fool God! That we weren't educating them out of their class in the least. We were educating them *into* their natural class much more effectually than is done in the average family. We weren't trying to force them into college if they hadn't any brains, as happens with rich men's sons; and we weren't putting them to work at fourteen if they were naturally ambitious, as happens with poor men's sons. We were watching them closely and individually and discovering their level. If our children showed an aptitude to become farm laborers and nurse-maids, we were going to teach them to be the best possible farm laborers and nurse-maids; and if they showed a tendency to become lawyers, we would turn them into honest, intelligent, open-minded lawyers. (He's a lawyer himself, but certainly not an open-minded one.)

He grunted when I had finished my remarks, and stirred his tea vigorously. Whereupon I suggested that perhaps he needed another lump of sugar, and dropped it in, and left him to absorb it.

The only way to deal with trustees is with a firm and steady hand. You have to keep them in their places.

Oh, my dear! that smudge in the corner was caused by Singapore's black tongue. He is trying to send you an affectionate kiss. Poor Sing thinks he's a lap dog—isn't it a tragedy when people mistake their vocations? I myself am not always certain that I was born an orphan-asylum superintendent.

Yours, til deth,
S. McB.

SUPERINTENDENT'S OFFICE,
JOHN GRIER HOME,
April 4.

THE PENDLETON FAMILY,
Palm Beach, Florida.

Dear Sir and Madam:

I have weathered my first visitors' day, and made the trustees a beautiful speech. Everybody said it was a beautiful speech—even my enemies.

Mr. Gordon Hallock's recent visit was exceptionally opportune; I gleaned from him many suggestions as to how to carry an audience.

"Be funny."—I told about Sadie Kate and a few other cherubs that you don't know.

"Keep it concrete and fitted to the intelligence of your audience."—I watched the Hon. Cy, and never said a thing that he couldn't understand.

"Flatter your hearers."—I hinted delicately that all of these new reforms were due to the wisdom and initiative of our peerless trustees.

"Give it a high moral tone, with a dash of pathos."—I dwelt upon the parentless condition of these little wards of Society. And it was very affecting—my enemy wiped away a tear!

Then I fed them up on chocolate and whipped cream and lemonade and tartar sandwiches, and sent them home, expansive and beaming, but without any appetite for dinner.

I dwell thus at length upon our triumph, in order to

70

create in you a happy frame of mind, before passing to the hideous calamity that so nearly wrecked the occasion.

> "Now follows the dim horror of my tale,
> And I feel I'm growing gradually pale,
>   For, even at this day,
>   Though its smell has passed away,
> When I venture to remember it, I quail!"

You never heard of our little Tammas Kehoe, did you? I simply haven't featured Tammas because he requires so much ink and time and vocabulary. He's a spirited lad, and he follows his dad, a mighty hunter of old—that sounds like more Bab Ballads, but it isn't; I made it up as I went along.

We can't break Tammas of his inherited predatory instincts. He shoots the chickens with bows and arrows and lassoes the pigs and plays bull-fight with the cows—and oh, is very destructive! But his crowning villainy occurred an hour before the trustees' meeting, when we wanted to be so clean and sweet and engaging.

It seems that he had stolen the rat-trap from the oat-bin, and had set it up in the wood lot, and yesterday morning was so fortunate as to catch a fine big skunk.

Singapore was the first to report the discovery. He returned to the house and rolled on the rugs in a frenzy of remorse over his part of the business. While our attention was occupied with Sing, Tammas was busily skinning his prey in the seclusion of the wood-shed. He buttoned the pelt inside his jacket, conveyed it by a devious route through the length of this building, arid concealed it under his bed where he thought it wouldn't be found. Then he went—per schedule—to the basement to help freeze the ice-cream for our guests. You notice that we omitted ice-cream from the menu.

In the short time that remained we created all the counter-irritation that was possible. Noah (negro furnace man) started smudge fires at intervals about the grounds. Cook waved a shovelful of burning coffee through the house. Betsy sprinkled the corridors with ammonia. Miss Snaith daintily treated the rugs with violet water. I sent an emergency call to the doctor, who came and mixed a gigantic solution of chloride of lime. But still, above and beneath and through every other odor, the unlaid ghost of Tammas's victim cried for vengeance.

The first business that came up at the meeting, was whether we should dig a hole and bury, not only Tammas, but the whole main building. You can see with what finesse I carried off the shocking event, when I tell you that the Hon. Cy went home chuckling over a funny story, instead of grumbling at the new superintendent's inability to manage boys.

We've our ain bit weird to dree!

As ever,
S. McBride.

Dear Judy:

Singapore is still living in the carriage house, and receiving a daily carbolic-scented bath from Tammas Kehoe. I am hoping that some day, in the distant future, my darling will be fit to return.

You will be pleased to hear that I have instituted a new method of spending your money. We are henceforth to buy a part of our shoes and dry-goods and drug-store comestibles from local shops, at not quite such low prices as the wholesale jobbers give, but still at a discount, and the education that is being thrown in is worth the difference. The reason is this: I have made the discovery that half of my children know nothing of money or its purchasing power. They think that shoes and corn-meal and red-flannel petticoats and mutton stew and gingham shirts just float down from the blue sky.

Last week I dropped a new green dollar bill out of my purse, and an eight-year-old urchin picked it up and asked if he could keep that picture of a bird. (American eagle in the center.) That child had never seen a bill in his life! I began an investigation, and discovered that dozens of children in this asylum have never bought anything or have ever seen anybody buy anything. And we are planning to turn them out at sixteen into a world governed entirely by the purchasing power of dollars and cents! Good heavens! just think of it! They are not to lead sheltered lives with somebody eternally looking after them; they have got to know how to get the very most they can out of every penny they can manage to earn.

I pondered the question all one night, at intervals, and went to the village at nine o'clock the next morning. I held conferences with seven storekeepers; found four open-minded and helpful, two doubtful, and one actively stupid. I have started with the four—dry-goods, groceries, shoes, and stationery. In return for somewhat large orders from us, they are to turn themselves and their clerks into teachers for my children, who are to go to the stores, inspect the stocks, and do their own purchasing with real money.

For example, Jane needs a spool of blue sewing-silk and a yard of elastic; so two little girls, intrusted with a silver quarter, trot hand in hand to Mr. Meeker's. They match the silk with anxious care, and watch the clerk jealously while he measures the elastic, to make sure that he doesn't stretch it. Then they bring back six cents change, receive my thanks and praise, and retire to the ranks tingling with a sense of achievement.

Isn't it pathetic? Ordinary children of ten or twelve automatically know so many things that our little incubator chicks have never dreamed of. But I have a variety of plans on foot. Just give me time, and you will see. One of these days I'll be turning out some nearly normal youngsters.

LATER.

I've an empty evening ahead, so I'll settle to some further gossip with you.

You remember the peanuts that Gordon Hallock sent? Well, I was so gracious when I thanked him that it incited him to fresh effort. He apparently went into a toy shop, and placed himself unreservedly in the hands of an enterprising clerk. Yesterday two husky expressmen deposited in our front hall a crate full of expensive furry animals built to be consumed by the children of the rich. They are not exactly what I should have purchased had I been the one to disburse such a fortune, but my babies find them very huggable. The chicks are now taking to bed with them lions and elephants and bears and giraffes. I don't know what the psychological effect will be. Do you suppose when they grow up they will all join the circus?

Oh, dear me, here is Miss Snaith, coming to pay a social call.

Good-by.

S.

P.S. The prodigal has returned. He sends his respectful regards, and three wags of the tail.

My dear Judy:

I have just been reading a pamphlet on manual training for girls, and another on the proper diet for institutions—right proportions of proteins, fats, starches, etc. In these days of scientific charity, when every problem has been tabulated, you can run an institution by chart. I don't see how Mrs. Lippett could have made all the mistakes she did, assuming, of course, that she knew how to read. But there is one quite important branch of institutional work that has not been touched upon, and I myself am gathering data. Some day I shall issue a pamphlet on the "Management and Control of Trustees."

I must tell you the joke about my enemy—not the Hon. Cy, but my first, my original enemy. He has undertaken a new field of endeavor. He says quite soberly (everything he does is sober; he has never smiled yet) that he has been watching me closely since my arrival, and though I am untrained and foolish and flippant (sic), he doesn't think that I am really so superficial as I at first appeared. I have an almost masculine ability of grasping the whole of a question and going straight to the point.

Aren't men funny? When they want to pay you the greatest compliment in their power, they naïvely tell you that you have a masculine mind. There is one compliment, incidentally, that I shall never be paying him. I cannot honestly say that he has a quickness of perception almost feminine.

So, though Sandy quite plainly sees my faults, still, he

76

thinks that some of them may be corrected; and he has determined to carry on my education from the point where the college dropped it. A person in my position ought to be well read in physiology, biology, psychology, sociology, and eugenics; she should know the hereditary effects of insanity, idiocy, and alcohol; should be able to administer the Binet test; and should understand the nervous system of a frog. In pursuance whereof, he has placed at my disposal his own scientific library of four thousand volumes. He not only fetches in the books he wants me to read, but comes and asks questions to make sure I haven't skipped.

We devoted last week to the life and letters of the Jukes family. Margaret, the mother of criminals, six generations ago, founded a prolific line, and her progeny, mostly in jail, now numbers some twelve hundred. Moral: watch the children with a bad heredity so carefully that none of them can ever have any excuse for growing up into Jukeses.

So now, as soon as we have finished our tea, Sandy and I get out the Doomsday Book, and pore over its pages in an anxious search for alcoholic parents. It's a cheerful little game to while away the twilight hour after the day's work is done.

Quelle vie! Come home fast and take me out of it. I'm wearying for the sight of you.

SALLIE.

My dear Pendleton Family:

I have received your letter, and I seize my pen to stop you. I don't wish to be relieved. I take it back. I change my mind. The person you are planning to send sounds like an exact twin of Miss Snaith. How can you ask me to turn over my darling children to a kind, but ineffectual, middle-aged lady without any chin? The very thought of it wrings a mother's heart.

Do you imagine that such a woman can carry on this work even temporarily? No! The manager of an institution like this has got to be young and husky and energetic and forceful and efficient and red-haired and sweet-tempered, like me. Of course I've been discontented,—anybody would be with things in such a mess,—but it's what you socialists call a holy discontent. And do you think that I am going to abandon all of the beautiful reforms I have so pains-takingly started? No! I am not to be moved from this spot until you find a superintendent superior to Sallie McBride.

That does not mean, though, that I am mortgaging myself forever. Just for the present, until things get on their feet. While the face-washing, airing, reconstructing period lasts, I honestly believe you chose the right person when you hit upon me. I *love* to plan improvements and order people about.

This is an awfully messy letter, but I'm dashing it off in three minutes in order to catch you before you definitely engage that pleasant, inefficient middle-aged person with-out a chin.

78

Please, kind lady and gentleman, don't do me out of me job! Let me stay a few months longer. Just gimme a chance to show what I'm good for, and I promise you won't never regret it.

S. McB.

Dear Judy:
I've composed a poem—a pæan of victory.

Robin MacRae
Smiled to-day.

It's the truth!

S. McB.

Dear Judy:

I am gratified to learn that you were gratified to learn that I am going to stay. I hadn't realized it, but I am really getting sort of attached to orphans.

It's an awful disappointment that Jervis has business which will keep you South so much longer. I am bursting with talk, and it is such a laborious nuisance having to write everything I want to say.

Of course I am glad that we are to have the building remodeled, and I think all of your ideas good, but I have a few extra good ones myself. It will be nice to have the new gymnasium and sleeping-porches, but, oh, my soul does long for cottages! The more I look into the internal workings of an orphan-asylum, the more I realize that the only type of asylum that can compete with a private family is one on the cottage system. So long as the family is the unit of society, children should be hardened early to family life.

The problem that is keeping me awake at present is, What to do with the children while we are being made over? It is hard to live in a house and build it at the same time. How would it be if I rented a circus tent and pitched it on the lawn?

Also, when we plunge into our alterations, I want a few guest-rooms where our children can come back when ill or out of work. The great secret of our lasting influence in their lives will be our watchful care afterward. What a terribly *alone* feeling it must give a person not to have a family hovering in the background! With all my dozens of aunts and uncles and mothers and fathers and cousins and brothers and sisters, I can't visualize it. I'd be terrified and panting if I didn't have lots of cover to run to. And for these forlorn little mites, somehow or other the John Grier Home must supply their need. So, dear people, send me half a dozen guest-rooms, if you please.

Good-by, and I'm glad you didn't put in the other woman. The very suggestion of somebody else taking over my own beautiful reforms before they were even started, stirred up all the opposition in me. I'm afraid I'm like Sandy—I canna think aught is dune richt except my ain hand is in 't.

Yours, for the present,
SALLIE MCBRIDE.

Dear Gordon:

I know that I haven't written lately; you have a perfect right to grumble, but oh dear! oh dear! you can't imagine what a busy person an orphan-asylum superintendent is. And all the writing energy I possess has to be expended upon that voracious Judy Abbott Pendleton. If three days go by without a letter, she telegraphs to know if the asylum has burned; whereas, if you—nice man—go letterless, you simply send us a present to remind us of your existence. So, you see, it's distinctly to our advantage to slight you often.

You will probably be annoyed when I tell you that I have promised to stay on here. They finally did find a woman to take my place, but she wasn't at all the right type and would have answered only temporarily. And, my dear Gordon, it's true, when I faced saying good-by to this feverish planning and activity, Worcester somehow looked rather colorless. I couldn't bear to let my asylum go unless I was sure of substituting a life packed equally full of sensation.

I know the alternative you will suggest, but please don't—just now. I told you before that I must have a few months longer to make up my mind. And in the meantime I like the feeling that I'm of use in the world. There's something constructive and optimistic about working with children; that is, if you look at it from my cheerful point of view, and not from our Scotch doctor's. I've never seen anybody like that man; he's always pessimistic and morbid

and down. It's best not to be too intelligent about insanity
and dipsomania and all the other hereditary details. I am
just about ignorant enough to be light-hearted and effective in a place like this.

The thought of all of these little lives expanding in
every direction eternally thrills me; there are so many
possibilities in our child garden for every kind of flower. It
has been planted rather promiscuously, to be sure, but
though we undoubtedly shall gather a number of weeds,
we are also hoping for some rare and beautiful blossoms.
Am I not growing sentimental? It is due to hunger—and
there goes the dinner-gong! We are going to have a delicious meal: roast beef and creamed carrots and beet greens,
with rhubarb pie for dessert. Would you not like to dine
with me? I should love to have you.

Most cordially yours,
S. McB.

P.S. You should see the number of poor homeless cats that
these children want to adopt. We had four when I came,
and they have all had kittens since. I haven't taken an
exact census, but I think the institution possesses nineteen.

Skimmed Milk
is served in the
Woodshed at 12 o'clock

My *dear Judy:*

You'd like to make another slight donation to the J. G. H. out of the excess of last month's allowance? *Bene!* Will you kindly have the following inserted in all low-class metropolitan dailies:

Notice!
To Parents Planning to Abandon their Children:
Please do it before they have reached their third year.

I can't think of any action on the part of abandoning parents that would help us more effectually. This having to root up evil before you begin planting good is slow, discouraging work.

We have one child here who has almost floored me; but I *will not* acknowledge myself beaten by a child of five. He alternates between sullen moroseness, when he won't speak a word, and the most violent out-bursts of temper, when he smashes everything within reach. He has been here only three months, and in that time he has destroyed nearly every piece of bric-à-brac in the institution—not, by the way, a great loss to art.

A month or so before I came he pulled the tablecloth from the officers' table while the girl in charge was in the corridor sounding the gong. The soup had already been served. You can imagine the mess! Mrs. Lippett half killed the child on that occasion, but the killing did nothing to lessen the temper, which was handed on to me intact.

His father was Italian and his mother Irish; he has red

hair and freckles from County Cork and the most beautiful
brown eyes that ever came out of Naples. After the father
was stabbed in a fight and the mother had died of alcoholism, the poor little chap by some chance or other got to
us; I suspect that he belongs in the Catholic Protectory.
As for his manners—oh dear! oh dear! They are what you
would expect. He kicks and bites and swears. I have
dubbed him Punch.

Yesterday he was brought squirming and howling to my
office, charged with having knocked down a little girl and
robbed her of her doll. Miss Snaith plumped him into
a chair behind me, and left him to grow quiet, while
I went on with my writing. I was suddenly startled by
an awful crash. He had pushed that big green jardinière
off the window-sill and broken it into five hundred
pieces. I jumped with a suddenness that swept the ink-
bottle to the floor, and when Punch saw that second
catastrophe, he stopped roaring with rage and threw
back his head and roared with laughter. The child is
diabolical.

I have determined to try a new method of discipline
that I don't believe in the whole of his forlorn little life he
has ever experienced. I am going to see what praise and
encouragement and love will do. So, instead of scolding
him about the jardinière, I assumed that it was an accident. I kissed him and told him not to feel bad; that I
didn't mind in the least. It shocked him into being quiet;
he simply held his breath and stared while I wiped away
his tears and sopped up the ink.

The child just now is the biggest problem that the
J. G. H. affords. He needs the most patient, loving,
individual care—a proper mother and father, likewise some

brothers and sisters and a grandmother. But I can't place
him in a respectable family until I make over his language
and his propensity to break things. I separated him from
the other children, and kept him in my room all the
morning, Jane having removed to safe heights all destruc-
tible *objets d'art*. Fortunately, he loves to draw, and he
sat on a rug for two hours, and occupied himself with
colored pencils. He was so surprised when I showed an
interest in a red-and-green ferry-boat, with a yellow
flag floating from the mast, that he became quite pro-
fanely affable. Until then I couldn't get a word out
of him.

In the afternoon Dr. MacRae dropped in and admired
the ferry-boat, while Punch swelled with the pride of
creation. Then, as a reward for being such a good little
boy, the doctor took him out in his automobile on a visit
to a country patient.

Punch was restored to the fold at five o'clock by a
sadder and wiser doctor. At a sedate country estate he had
stoned the chickens, smashed a cold frame, and swung the
pet Angora cat by its tail. Then when the sweet old lady
tried to make him be kind to poor pussy, he told her to go
to hell.

I can't bear to consider what some of these children
have seen and experienced. It will take years of sunshine
and happiness and love to eradicate the dreadful memories
that they have stored up in the far-back corners of their
little brains. And there are so many children and so few of
us that we can't hug them enough; we simply haven't
arms or laps to go around.

Mais parlons d'autres choses! Those awful questions
of heredity and environment that the doctor broods

Our little Punch
goes
visiting

over so constantly are getting into my blood, too; and it's a vicious habit. If a person is to be of any use in a place like this, she must see nothing but good in the world. Optimism is the only wear for a social worker.

" 'T is the middle of night by the castle clock"—do you know where that beautiful line of poetry comes from? "Cristabel," of English K. Mercy! how I hated that course! You, being an English shark, liked it; but I never understood a word that was said from the time I entered the class-room till I left it. However, the remark with which I opened this paragraph is true. It *is* the middle of night by the mantelpiece clock, so I'll wish you pleasant dreams.

Addio!
SALLIE.

Dear Enemy:

You doctored the whole house, then stalked past my library with your nose in the air, while I was waiting tea with a plate of Scotch scones sitting on the trivet, ordered expressly for you as a peace-offering.

If you really hurt, I will read the Kallikak book; but I must tell you that you are working me to death. It takes almost all of my energy to be an effective superintendent, and this university-extension course that you are conducting I find wearing. You remember how indignant you were one day last week because I confessed to having stayed up until one o'clock the night before? Well, my dear man, if I were to accomplish all the vicarious reading you require, I should sit up until morning every night.

However, bring it in. I usually manage half an hour of recreation after dinner, and though I had wanted to glance at Wells's latest novel, I will amuse myself instead with your feeble-minded family.

Life of late is unco steep.

Obligingly yours,
S. McB.

THE JOHN GRIER HOME,
April 17.

Dear Gordon:

Thank you for the tulips, likewise the lilies of the valley. They are most becoming to my blue Persian bowls.

Have you ever heard of the Kallikaks? Get the book and read them up. They are a two-branch family in New Jersey, I think, though their real name and origin is artfully concealed. But, anyway,—and this is true,—six generations ago a young gentleman, called for convenience Martin Kallikak, got drunk one night and temporarily eloped with a feeble-minded barmaid, thus founding a long line of feeble-minded Kallikaks,—drunkards, gamblers, prostitutes, horse thieves,—a scourge to New Jersey and surrounding States.

Martin later straightened up, married a normal woman, and founded a second line of proper Kallikaks,—judges, doctors, farmers, professors, politicians,—a credit to their country. And there the two branches still are, flourishing side by side. You can see what a blessing it would have been to New Jersey if something drastic had happened to that feeble-minded barmaid in her infancy.

It seems that feeble-mindedness is a very hereditary quality, and science isn't able to overcome it. No operation has been discovered for introducing brains into the head of a child who didn't start with them. And the child grows up with, say, a nine-year brain in a thirty-year body, and becomes an easy tool for any criminal he meets. Our prisons are one-third full of feeble-minded convicts. Society ought to segregate them on feeble-minded farms, where they can earn their livings in peaceful menial pursuits, and not have children. Then in a generation or so we might be able to wipe them out.

Did you know all that? It's very necessary information for a politician to have. Get the book and read it, please; I'd send my copy only that it's borrowed.

It's also very necessary information for me to have. There are eleven of these chicks that I suspect a bit, and I am *sure* of Loretta Higgins. I have been trying for a month to introduce one or two basic ideas into that child's brain, and now I know what the trouble is: her head is filled with a sort of soft cheesy substance instead of brain.

I came up here to make over this asylum in such little details as fresh air and food and clothes and sunshine, but, heavens! you can see what problems I am facing. I've got to make over society first, so that it won't send me sub-normal children to work with. Excuse all this excited conversation; but I've just met up with the subject of feeble-mindedness, and it's appalling—and interesting. It is your business as a legislator to make laws that will remove it from the world. Please attend to this immediately,

And oblige,

S. MCBRIDE,
Sup't John Grier Home.

Dear Man of Science:

You didn't come to-day. Please don't skip us tomorrow. I have finished the Kallikak family and I am bursting with talk. Don't you think we ought to have a psychologist examine these children? We owe it to adopting parents not to saddle them with feeble-minded offspring.

You know, I'm tempted to ask you to prescribe arsenic for Loretta's cold. I've diagnosed her case; she's a Kallikak. Is it right to let her grow up and found a line of 378 feeble-minded people for society to care for? Oh dear! I do hate to poison the child, but what can I do?

S. McB.

Dear Gordon:

You aren't interested in feeble-minded people, and you are shocked because I am? Well, I am equally shocked because you are not. If you aren't interested in everything of the sort that there unfortunately is in this world, how can you make wise laws? You can't.

However, at your request, I will converse upon a less morbid subject. I've just bought fifty yards of blue and rose and green and corn-colored hair-ribbon as an Easter present for my fifty little daughters. I am also thinking of sending you an Easter present. How would a nice fluffy little kitten please you? I can offer any of the following patterns:—

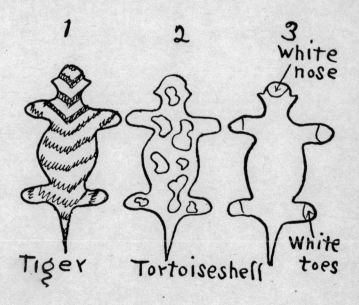

Number 3 comes in any color, gray, black, or yellow. If
you will let me know which you would rather have, I will
express it at once.

I would write a respectable letter, but it's tea-time, and
I see that a guest approaches.

Addio!
SALLIE.

P.S. Don't you know some one who would like to adopt a
desirable baby boy with seventeen nice new teeth?

April 20.

My *dear* Judy:

One a penny, two a penny, hot cross buns! We've had a Good Friday present of ten dozen, given by Mrs. De Peyster Lambert, a high-church, stained-glass-window soul whom I met at a tea a few days ago. (Who says now that teas are a silly waste of time?) She asked me about my "precious little waifs," and said I was doing a noble work and would be rewarded. I saw buns in her eye, and sat down and talked to her for half an hour.

Now I shall go and thank her in person, and tell her with a great deal of affecting detail how much those buns were appreciated by my precious little waifs—omitting the account of how precious little Punch threw his bun at Miss Snaith and plastered her neatly in the eye. I think, with encouragement, Mrs. De Peyster Lambert can be developed into a cheerful giver.

Oh, I'm growing into the most shocking beggar! My family don't dare to visit me, because I demand *bakshish* in such a brazen manner. I threatened to remove father from my calling-list unless he shipped immediately sixty-five pairs of overalls for my prospective gardeners. A notice from the freight office this morning asks me to remove two packing-cases consigned to them by the J. L. McBride Co. of Worcester; so I take it that father desires to continue my acquaintance. Jimmie hasn't sent us anything yet, and he's getting a huge salary. I write him frequently a pathetic list of our needs.

But Gordon Hallock has learned the way to a mother's heart. I was so pleasant about the peanuts and menagerie

97

that now he sends a present of some sort every few days, and I spend my entire time composing thank-you letters that aren't exact copies of the ones I've sent before. Last week we received a dozen big scarlet balls. The nursery is *full* of them; you kick them before you as you walk. And yesterday there arrived a half-bushel of frogs and ducks and fishes to float in the bath-tubs.

Send, O best of trustees, the tubs in which to float them!

I am, as usual,
S. MCBRIDE.

My dear Judy:

Spring must be lurking about somewhere; the birds are arriving from the South. Isn't it time you followed their example?

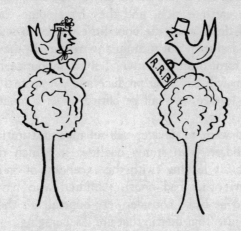

Society note from the *Bird o' Passage News*:

"Mr. and Mrs. First Robin have returned from a trip to Florida. It is hoped that Mr. and Mrs. Jervis Pendleton will arrive shortly."

Even up here in our dilatory Dutchess County the breeze smells green; it makes you want to be out and away, roaming the hills, or else down on your knees grubbing in the dirt. Isn't it funny what farmering instincts the budding spring awakens in even the most urban souls?

I have spent the morning making plans for little private gardens for every child over nine. The big potato-field is doomed. That is the only feasible spot for sixty-two private gardens. It is near enough to be watched from the north windows, and yet far enough away, so that their messing will not injure our highly prized landscape lawn. Also the earth is rich, and they have some chance of success. I don't want the poor little chicks to scratch all summer, and then not turn up any treasure in the end. In order to furnish an incentive, I shall announce that the institution will buy their produce and pay in real money, though I foresee we shall be buried under a mountain of radishes.

I do so want to develop self-reliance and initiative in these children, two sturdy qualities in which they are conspicuously lacking (with the exception of Sadie Kate and a few other bad ones). Children who have spirit enough to be bad I consider very hopeful; it's those who are good just from inertia that are discouraging.

The last few days have been spent mainly in charming the devil out of Punch, an interesting task if I could devote my whole time to it; but with one hundred and seven other little devils to charm away, my attention is sorely deflected.

The awful thing about this life is that whatever I am doing, the other things that I am not doing, but ought to be, keep tugging at my skirts. There is no doubt but Punch's personal devil needs the whole attention of a whole person,—preferably two persons,—so that they could spell each other and get some rest.

Sadie Kate has just flown in from the nursery with news of a scarlet gold-fish (Gordon's gift) swallowed by one of our babies. Mercy! the number of calamities that can occur in an orphan-asylum!

9 P.M.

My children are in bed, and I've just had a thought. Wouldn't it be heavenly if the hibernating system prevailed among the human young? There would be some pleasure in running an asylum if one could just tuck the little darlings into bed the first of October and keep them there until the twenty-second of April.

I'm yours, as ever,
SALLIE.

April 24.

Dear Jervis Pendleton Esq.:

This is to supplement a night telegram which I sent you ten minutes ago. Fifty words not being enough to convey any idea of my emotions, I herewith add a thousand.

As you will know by the time you receive this, I have discharged the farmer, and he has refused to be discharged. Being twice the size of me, I can't lug him to the gate and chuck him out. He wants a notification from the president of the board of trustees written in vigorous language on official paper in typewriting. So, dear president of the board of trustees, kindly supply all of this at your earliest convenience.

Here follows the history of the case:

The winter season still being with us when I arrived and farming activities at a low ebb, I have heretofore paid little attention to Robert Sterry except to note on two occasions that his pig-pens needed cleaning; but to-day I sent for him to come and consult with me in regard to spring planting.

Sterry came, as requested, and seated himself at ease in my office with his hat upon his head. I suggested as tactfully as might be that he remove it, an entirely necessary request, as little orphan boys were in and out on errands, and "hats off in the house" is our first rule in masculine deportment.

Sterry complied with my request, and stiffened himself to be against whatever I might desire.

I proceeded to the subject in hand, namely, that the diet of the John Grier Home in the year to come is to consist less exclusively of potatoes. At which our farmer grunted in the manner of the Hon. Cyrus Wykoff, only it

102

was a less ethereal and gentlemanly grunt than a trustee permits himself. I enumerated corn and beans and onions and peas and tomatoes and beets and carrots and turnips as desirable substitutes.

Sterry observed that if potatoes and cabbages was good enough for him, he guessed they was good enough for charity children.

I proceeded imperturbably to say that the two-acre potato-field was to be plowed and fertilized, and laid out into sixty individual gardens, the boys assisting in the work.

At that Sterry exploded. The two-acre field was the most fertile and valuable piece of earth on the whole place. He guessed if I was to break that up into play-gardens for the children to mess about in, I'd be hearing about it pretty danged quick from the board of trustees. That field was fitted for potatoes, it had always raised potatoes, and it was going to continue to raise them just as long as he had anything to say about it.

"You have nothing what ever to say about it," I amiably replied. "I have decided that the two-acre field is the best plot to use for the children's gardens, and you and the potatoes will have to give way."

Whereupon he rose in a storm of bucolic wrath, and said he'd be gol darned if he'd have a lot of these danged city brats interfering with his work.

I explained—very calmly for a red-haired person with Irish forebears—that this place was run for the exclusive benefit of these children; that the children were not here to be exploited for the benefit of the place, a philosophy which he did not grasp, though my fancy city language had a slightly dampening effect. I added that what I required in a farmer was the ability and patience to in-

struct the boys in gardening and simple outdoor work; that
I wished a man of large sympathies whose example would be
an inspiring influence to these children of the city streets.

Sterry, pacing about like a caged woodchuck, launched
into a tirade about silly Sunday-school notions, and, by a
transition which I did not grasp, passed to a review of the

general subject of woman's suffrage. I gathered that he is
not in favor of the movement. I let him argue himself quiet,
then I handed him a check for his wages, and told him to
vacate the tenant house by twelve o'clock next Wednesday.

Sterry says he'll be danged if he will. (Excuse so many
dangeds. It is the creature's only adjective.) He was engaged to work for this institution by the president of the
board of trustees, and he will not move from that house
until the president of the board of trustees tells him to go.
I don't think poor Sterry realizes that since his arrival a
new president has come to the throne.

Alors you have the story. I make no threats, but Sterry
or McBride—take your choice, dear sir.

I am also about to write to the head of the Massachusetts Agricultural College, at Amherst, asking him to
recommend a good, practical man with a nice, efficient,
cheerful wife, who will take the entire care of our modest
domain of seventeen acres, and who will be a man with
the right personality to place over our boys.

If we get the farming end of this institution into running shape, it ought to furnish not only beans and onions
for the table, but education for our hands and brains.

> I remain, sir,
> Yours most truly,
>   S. MCBRIDE,
>   Superintendent of the
>   John Grier Home.

P.S. I think that Sterry will probably come back some
night and throw rocks through the windows. Shall I have
them insured?

My dear Enemy:

You disappeared so quickly this afternoon that I had no chance to thank you, but the echoes of that discharge penetrated as far as my library. Also, I have viewed the debris. What on earth did you do to poor Sterry? Watching the purposeful set of your shoulders as you strode toward the carriage-house, I was filled with sudden compunction. I did not want the man murdered, merely reasoned with. I am afraid you were a little harsh.

However, your technic seems to have been effective. Report says that he has telephoned for a moving-wagon and that Mrs. Sterry is even now on her hands and knees ripping up the parlor carpet.

For this relief much thanks.

SALLIE MCBRIDE.

106

Dear Jervis:

Your vigorous telegram was, after all, not needed. Dr. Robin MacRae, who is a grand *pawky* mon when it comes to a fight, accomplished the business with beautiful directness. I was so bubbling with rage that immediately after writing to you I called up the doctor on the telephone, and rehearsed the whole business over again. Now, our Sandy, whatever his failings (and he has them), does have an uncommon supply of common sense. He knows how useful those gardens are going to be, and how worse than useless Sterry was. Also says he, "The superintendent's authority must be upheld." (That, incidentally, is beautiful, coming from him.) But anyway, those were his words. And he hung up the receiver, cranked up his car, and flew up here at lawless speed. He marched straight to Sterry, impelled by a fine Scotch rage, and he discharged the man with such vigor and precision, that the carriage-house window was shattered to fragments.

Since this morning at eleven, when Sterry's wagonload of furniture rumbled out of the gates, a sweet peace has reigned over the J. G. H. A man from the village is helping us out while we hopefully await the farmer of our dreams.

I am sorry to have troubled you with our troubles. Tell Judy that she owes me a letter, and won't hear from me until she has paid it.

Your ob'd't servant,
S. McBride.

Dear Judy:

In my letter of yesterday to Jervis I forgotted (Punch's word) to convey to you our thanks for three tin bath-tubs. The sky-blue tub with poppies on the side adds a particularly bright note to the nursery. I do love presents for the babies that are too big to be swallowed.

You will be pleased to hear that our manual training is well under way. The carpenter-benches are being installed in the old primary room, and until our school-house gets its new addition, our primary class is meeting on the front porch, in accordance with Miss Matthews' able suggestion.

The girls' sewing-classes are also in progress. A circle of benches under the copper beech-tree accommodates the hand sewers, while the big girls take turns at our three machines. Just as soon as they gain some proficiency we will begin the glorious work of redressing the institution. I know you think I'm slow, but it's really a task to accomplish one hundred and eighty new frocks. And the girls will appreciate them so much more if they do the work themselves.

I may also report that our hygiene system has risen to a high level. Dr. MacRae has introduced morning and evening exercises, and a glass of milk and a game of tag in the middle of school hours. He has instituted a physiology class, and has separated the children into small groups, so that they may come to his house, where he has a manikin that comes apart and shows all its messy insides. They can now rattle off scientific truths about their little digestions as fluently as Mother-Goose rhymes. We are really becoming too intelligent for recognition. You would never guess that we were orphans to hear us talk; we are quite like Boston children.

108

2 P.M.

O Judy, such a calamity! Do you remember several
weeks ago I told you about placing out a nice little girl in
a nice family home where I hoped she would be adopted?
It was a kind Christian family living in a pleasant country
village, the foster-father a deacon in the church. Hattie
was a sweet, obedient, housewifely little body, and it
looked as though we had exactly fitted them to each
other. My dear, she was returned this morning for *stealing*.
Scandal piled on scandal: *she had stolen a communion-cup
from church!*

Between her sobs and their accusations it took me half
an hour to gather the truth. It seems that the church they
attend is very modern and hygienic, like our doctor, and
has introduced individual communion-cups. Poor little Hattie had never heard of communion in her life; in fact, she
wasn't very used to church, Sunday-school having always
sufficed for her simple religious needs. But in her new
home she attended both, and one day, to her pleased
surprise, they served refreshments. But they skipped her.
She made no comment, however; she is used to being
skipped. But as they were starting home she saw that the
little silver cup had been casually left in the seat, and
supposing that it was a souvenir that you could take if you
wished, she put it into her pocket.

It came to light two days later as the most treasured
ornament of her doll's-house. It seems that Hattie long
ago saw a set of doll's-dishes in a toy-shop window, and
has ever since dreamed of possessing a set of her own. The
communion-cup was not quite the same, but it answered.
Now, if our family had only had a little less religion

and a little more sense, they would have returned the
cup, perfectly unharmed, and have marched Hattie to
the nearest toy-shop and bought her some dishes. But
instead, they bundled the child and her belongings into
the first train they could catch, and shoved her in
at our front door, proclaiming loudly that she was a
thief.

I am pleased to say that I gave that indignant deacon
and his wife such a thorough scolding as I am sure they
have never listened to from the pulpit; I borrowed some
vigorous bits from Sandy's vocabulary, and sent them
home quite humbled. As for poor little Hattie, here she is
back again, after going out with such high hopes. It has an
awfully bad moral effect on a child to be returned to the
asylum in disgrace, especially when she wasn't aware of
committing a crime. It gives her a feeling that the world is
full of unknown pitfalls, and makes her afraid to take a
step. I must bend all my energies now toward finding
another set of parents for her, and ones that haven't
grown so old and settled and good that they have entirely
forgotten their own childhood.

                                              Sunday.

I forgot to tell you that our new farmer is here, Turnfelt
by name; and his wife is a love, yellow hair and dimples. If
she were an orphan, I could place her in a minute. We
can't let her go to waste. I have a beautiful plan of
building an addition to the farmer's cottage, and establish-
ing under her comfortable care a sort of brooding-house
where we can place our new little chicks, to make sure
they haven't anything contagious and to eliminate as

much profanity as possible before turning them loose among our other perfect chicks.

How does that strike you? It is very necessary in an institution as full of noise and movement and stir as this to have some isolated spot where we can put cases needing individual attention. Some of our children have inherited nerves, and a period of quiet contemplation is indicated. Isn't my vocabulary professional and scientific? Daily intercourse with Dr. Robin MacRae is extremely educational.

Since Turnfelt came, you should see our pigs. They are so clean and pink and unnatural that they don't recognize one another any more as they pass.

Our potato-field is also unrecognizable. It has been divided with string and pegs into as many squares as a checker-board, and every child has staked out a claim. Seed catalogues form our only reading matter.

Noah has just returned from a trip to the village for the Sunday papers to amuse his leisure. Noah is a very cultivated person; he not only reads perfectly, but he wears tortoise-shell-rimmed spectacles while he does it. He also brought from the post-office a letter from you, written Friday night. I am pained to note that you do not care for "Gösta Berling" and that Jervis doesn't. The only comment I can make is, "What a shocking lack of literary taste in the Pendleton family!"

Dr. MacRae has another doctor visiting him, a very melancholy gentleman who is at the head of a private psychopathic institution, and thinks there's no good in life. But I suppose this pessimistic view is natural if you eat three meals a day with a tableful of melancholics. He goes up and down the world looking for signs of degeneracy, and finds them everywhere. I expected, after half an hour's conversation, that he would ask to look down my throat to see if I had a cleft palate. Sandy's taste in friends seems to resemble his taste in literature.

Gracious! this is a letter!

Good-by.
SALLIE.

Thursday, May 2.

Dear Judy:

Such a bewildering whirl of events! The J. G. H. is breathless. Incidentally, I am on the way toward solving my problem of what to do with the children while the carpenters and plumbers and masons are here. Or, rather, my precious brother has solved it for me.

This afternoon I went over my linen supply, and made the shocking discovery that we have only sheets enough to change the children's beds every two weeks, which, it appears, is our shiftless custom. While I was still in the midst of my household gear, with a bunch of keys at my girdle, looking like the chatelaine of a medieval château, who should be ushered in but Jimmie?

Being extremely occupied, I dropped a slanting kiss on his nose, and sent him off to look over the place in charge of my two oldest urchins. They collected six friends and organized a base-ball game. Jimmie came back blown, but enthusiastic, and consented to prolong his visit over the week-end, though after the dinner I gave him he has decided to take his future meals at the hotel. As we sat with our coffee before the fire, I confided to him my anxiety as to what should be done with the chicks while their new brooder is building. You know Jimmie. In one half a minute his plan was formulated.

"Build an Adirondack camp on that little plateau up by the wood-lot. You can make three open shacks, each holding eight bunks, and move the twenty-four oldest boys out there for the summer. It won't cost two cents."

113

"Yes," I objected, "but it will cost more than two cents to engage a man to look after them."

"Perfectly easy," said Jimmie, grandly. "I'll find you a college fellow who'll be glad to come during the vacation for his board and a mere pittance, only you'll have to set up more filling board than you gave me to-night."

Dr. MacRae dropped in about nine o'clock, after visiting the hospital ward. We've got three cases of whooping-cough, but all isolated, and no more coming. How those three got in is a mystery. It seems there is a little bird that brings whooping-cough to orphan-asylums.

Jimmie fell upon him for backing in his camp scheme, and the doctor gave it enthusiastically. They seized pencil and paper and drew up plans; and before the evening was over, the last nail was hammered. Nothing would satisfy those two men but to go to the telephone at ten o'clock and rouse a poor carpenter from his sleep. He and some lumber are ordered for eight in the morning.

I finally got rid of them at ten-thirty, still talking uprights and joists and drainage and roof slants.

The excitement of Jimmie and coffee and all these building operations induced me to sit down immediately and write a letter to you; but I think, by your leave, I'll postpone further details to another time.

Yours ever,
SALLIE.

Dear Enemy:

Will you be after dining with us at seven to-night? It's a real dinner-party; we're going to have ice-cream.

My brother has discovered a promising young man to take charge of the boys,—maybe you know him,—Mr. Witherspoon, at the bank. I wish to introduce him to asylum circles by easy steps, so *please* don't mention insanity or epilepsy or alcoholism, or any of your other favorite topics.

He is a gay young society leader, used to very fancy things to eat. Do you suppose we can ever make him happy at the John Grier Home?

Yours in evident haste,
SALLIE MCBRIDE.

Sunday.

Dear Judy:

Jimmie was back at eight Friday morning, and the doctor at a quarter past. They and the carpenter and our new farmer and Noah and our two horses and our eight biggest boys have been working ever since. Never were building operations set going in faster time. I wish I had a dozen Jimmies on the place, though I will say that my brother works faster if you catch him before the first edge of his enthusiasm wears away. He would not be much good at chiseling out a medieval cathedral.

He came back Saturday morning aglow with a new idea. He had met at the hotel the night before a friend who belongs to his hunting-club in Canada, and who is cashier of our First (and only) National Bank.

"He's a bully good sport," said Jimmie, "and exactly the man you want to camp out with those kids and lick 'em into shape. He'll be willing to come for his board and forty dollars a month, because he's engaged to a girl in Detroit and wants to save. I told him the food was rotten, but if he kicked enough, you'd probably get a new cook."

"What's his name?" said I, with guarded interest.

"He's got a peach of a name. It's Percy de Forest Witherspoon."

I nearly had hysterics. Imagine a Percy de Forest Witherspoon in charge of those twenty-four wild little savages!

But you know Jimmie when he has an idea. He had already invited Mr. Witherspoon to dine with me on Saturday evening, and had ordered oysters and squabs and

116

ice-cream from the village caterer to help out my veal. It
ended by my giving a very formal dinner-party, with Miss
Matthews and Betsy and the doctor included.

I almost asked the Hon. Cy and Miss Snaith. Ever since
I have known those two, I have felt that there ought to be
a romance between them. Never have I known two people
who matched so perfectly. He's a widower with five children. Don't you suppose it might be arranged? If he had a
wife to take up his attention, it might deflect him a little
from us. I'd be getting rid of them both at one stroke. It's
to be considered among our future improvements.

Anyway, we had our dinner. And during the course of
the evening my anxiety grew, not as to whether Percy
would do for us, but as to whether we should do for Percy.
If I searched the world over, I never could find a young
man more calculated to win the affection of those boys.
You know, just by looking at him, that he does everything
well, at least everything vigorous. His literary and artistic
accomplishments I suspect a bit, but he rides and shoots
and plays golf and foot-ball and sails a boat. He likes to
sleep out of doors and he likes boys. He has always wanted
to know some orphans; often read about 'em in books, he
says, but never met any face to face. Percy does seem too
good to be true.

Before they left, Jimmie and the doctor hunted up a
lantern, and in their evening clothes conducted Mr.
Witherspoon across a plowed field to inspect his future
dwelling.

And such a Sunday as we passed! I had absolutely to
forbid their carpentering. Those men would have put in a
full day, quite irrespective of the damage done to one
hundred and four little moral natures. As it is, they have

just stood and looked at those shacks and handled their hammers, and thought about where they would drive the first nail to-morrow morning. The more I study men, the more I realize that they are nothing in the world but boys grown too big to be spankable.

I am awfully worried as to how to feed Mr. Witherspoon. He looks as though he had a frightfully healthy appetite, and he looks as though he couldn't swallow his dinner unless he had on evening clothes. I've made Betsy send home for a trunkful of evening gowns in order to keep up our social standing. One thing is fortunate: he takes his luncheon at the hotel, and I hear their luncheons are very filling.

Tell Jervis I am sorry he is not with us to drive a nail for the camp. Here comes the Hon. Cy up the path. Heaven save us!

Ever your unfortunate,
S. McB.

Dear Judy:

Our camp is finished, our energetic brother has gone, and our twenty-four boys have passed two healthful nights in the open. The three bark-covered shacks add a pleasant rustic touch to the grounds. They are like those we used to have in the Adirondacks, closed on three sides and open in the front, and one larger than the rest to allow a private pavilion for Mr. Percy Witherspoon. An adjacent hut, less exposed to the weather, affords extremely adequate bathing facilities, consisting of a faucet in the wall and three watering-cans. Each camp has a bath-master who stands on a stool and sprinkles each little shiverer as he trots under. Since our trustees *won't* give us enough bath-tubs, we have to use our wits.

The three camps have organized into three tribes of Indians, each with a chief of its own to answer for its conduct, Mr. Witherspoon high chief of all, and Dr. MacRae the medicine man. They dedicated their lodges Tuesday evening with appropriate tribal ceremonies; and though they politely invited me to attend, I decided that it was a purely masculine affair, so I declined to go, but sent refreshments, a very popular move. Betsy and I walked as far as the base-ball-field in the course of the evening, and caught a glimpse of the orgies. The braves were squatting in a circle about a big fire, each decorated with a blanket from his bed and a rakish band of feathers. (Our chickens seem very scant as to tail, but I have asked no unpleasant questions.) The doctor, with a Navajo blanket about his

119

shoulders, was executing a war-dance, while Jimmie and Mr. Witherspoon beat on war-drums—two of our copper kettles, now permanently dented. Fancy Sandy! It's the first youthful glimmer I have ever caught in the man.

After ten o'clock, when the braves were safely stowed for the night, the three men came in and limply dropped into comfortable chairs in my library, with the air of having made martyrs of themselves in the great cause of charity. But they did not deceive me. They originated all that tomfoolery for their own individual delectation.

So far Mr. Percy Witherspoon appears fairly happy. He is presiding at one end of the officers' table under the special protection of Betsy, and I am told that he instils considerable life into that sedate assemblage. I have endeavored to run up their menu a trifle, and he accepts what is put before him with a perfectly good appetite, irrespective of the absence of such accustomed trifles as oysters and quail and soft-shell crabs.

There was no sign of a private sitting-room that I could put at this young man's disposal, but he himself has solved the difficulty by proposing to occupy our new laboratory. So he spends his evenings with a book and a pipe, comfortably stretched in the dentist's chair. There are not many society men who would be willing to spend their evenings so harmlessly. That girl in Detroit is a lucky young thing.

Mercy! An automobile full of people has just arrived to look over the institution, and Betsy, who usually does the honors, not here. I fly.

Addio!
SALLIE.

My dear Gordon:

This is not a letter,—I don't owe you one,—it's a receipt for sixty-five pairs of roller-skates.

Many thanks.
S. McB.

Dear Enemy:

I hear that I missed a call to-day, but Jane delivered your message, together with the "Genetic Philosophy of Education." She says that you will call in a few days for my opinion of the book. Is it to be a written or an oral examination?

And doesn't it ever occur to you that this education business is rather one-sided? It often strikes me that Dr. Robin MacRae's mental attitude would also be the better for some slight refurbishing. I will promise to read your book, provided you read one of mine. I am sending herewith the "Dolly Dialogues," and shall ask for an opinion in a day or so.

It's uphill work making a Scotch Presbyterian frivolous, but persistency accomplishes wonders.

S. McB.

May 13.

My *dear, dear* Judy:

Talk about floods in Ohio! Right here in Dutchess
County we are the consistency of a wet sponge. Rain for
five days, and everything wrong with this institution.

The babies have had croup, and we have been up o'
nights with them. Cook has given notice, and there's a
dead rat in the walls. Our three camps leaked, and in the
early dawn, after the first cloud-burst, twenty-four bedrag-
gled little Indians, wrapped in damp bedding, came shiv-
ering to the door and begged for admission. Since then
every clothes-line, every stair-railing has been covered with
wet and smelly blankets that steam, but won't dry. Mr.
Percy de Forest Witherspoon has returned to the hotel to
wait until the sun comes out.

After being cooped up for four days with no exercise to
speak of, the children's badness is breaking out in red
spots, like the measles. Betsy and I have thought of every
form of active and innocent occupation that could be
carried on in such a congested quarter as this: blind-man's-
buff and pillow fights and hide-and-go-seek, gymnastics
in the dining-room, and bean-bags in the school-room.
(We broke two windows.) The boys played leap-frog up
and down the hall, and jarred all the plaster in the
building. We have cleaned energetically and furiously. All
the woodwork has been washed, and all of the floors
polished; but despite everything, we have a great deal of
energy left, and we are getting to that point of nerves
where we want to punch one another.

Sadie Kate has been acting like a little deil—do they

123

have feminine deils? If not, Sadie Kate has originated the species. And this afternoon Loretta Higgins had— well, I don't know whether it was a sort of fit or just a temper. She lay down on the floor and howled for a solid hour, and when any one tried to approach her, she thrashed about like a little wind-mill and bit and kicked.

By the time the doctor came she had pretty well worn herself out. He picked her up, limp and drooping, and carried her to a cot in the hospital-room; and after she was asleep he came down to my library and asked to look at the archives.

Loretta is thirteen; in the three years she has been here she has had five of these outbreaks, and has been punished good and hard for them. The child's ancestral record is simple: "Mother died of alcoholic dementia, Bloomingdale Asylum. Father unknown."

He studied the page long and frowningly and shook his head.

"With a heredity like that, is it right to punish the child for having a shattered nervous system?"

"It is not," said I, firmly. "We will mend her shattered nervous system."

"If we can."

"We'll feed her up on cod-liver oil and sunshine, and find a nice kind foster-mother who will take pity on the poor little—"

But then my voice trailed off into nothing as I pictured Loretta's face, with her hollow eyes and big nose and open mouth and no chin and stringy hair and sticking-out ears. No foster-mother in the world would love a child who looked like that.

"Why, oh, why," I wailed, "doesn't the good Lord send orphan children with blue eyes and curly hair and loving dispositions? I could place a million of that sort in kind homes, but no one wants Loretta."

"I'm afraid the good Lord doesn't have anything to do with bringing our Lorettas into the world. It is the devil who attends to them."

Poor Sandy! He gets awfully pessimistic about the future of the universe; but I don't wonder, with such a cheerless life as he leads. He looked to-day as though his own nervous system was shattered. He had been splashing about in the rain since five this morning, when he was called to a sick-baby case. I made him sit down and have some tea, and we had a nice, cheerful talk on drunkenness and idiocy and epilepsy and insanity. He dislikes alcoholic parents, but he ties himself into a knot over insane parents.

Privately, I don't believe there's one thing in heredity, provided you snatch the babies away before their eyes are opened. We've got the sunniest youngster here you ever saw; his mother and Aunt Ruth and Uncle Silas all died insane, but he is as placid and unexcitable as a cow.

Good-by, my dear. I am sorry this is not a more cheerful letter, though at this moment nothing unpleasant seems to be happening. It's eleven o'clock, and I have just stuck my head into the corridor, and all is quiet except for two banging shutters and leaking eaves. I promised Jane I would go to bed at ten.

Good night, and joy be wi' ye baith!
SALLIE.

P.S. There is one thing in the midst of all my troubles that I have to be grateful for: the Hon. Cy has been stricken with a lingering attack of grippe. In a burst of thankfulness I sent him a bunch of violets.

P.S. 2. We are having an epidemic of pink-eye.

Good morning, my dear Judy!

Three days of sunshine, and the J. G. H. is smiling.

I am getting my immediate troubles nicely settled. Those beastly blankets have dried at last, and our camps have been made livable again. They are floored with wooden slats and roofed with tar-paper. (Mr. Witherspoon calls them chicken-coops.) We are digging a stone-lined ditch to convey any further cloudbursts from the plateau on which they stand to the corn-field below. The Indians have resumed savage life, and their chief is back at his post.

The doctor and I have been giving Loretta Higgins's nerves our most careful consideration. We think that this barrack life, with its constant movement and stir, is too exciting, and we have decided that the best plan will be to board her out in a private family, where she will receive a great deal of individual attention.

The doctor, with his usual resourcefulness, has produced the family. They live next door to him and are very nice people; I have just returned from calling. The husband is foreman of the casting-room at the iron works, and the wife is a comfortable soul who shakes all over when she laughs. They live mostly in their kitchen in order to keep the parlor neat; but it is such a cheerful kitchen that I should like to live in it myself. She has potted begonias in the window and a nice purry tiger cat asleep on a braided rug in front of the stove. She bakes on Saturday—cookies and gingerbread and doughnuts. I am planning to pay my weekly call upon Loretta every Satur-

day morning at eleven o'clock. Apparently I made as
favorable an impression on Mrs. Wilson as she made on
me. After I had gone, she confided to the doctor that she
liked me because I was just as common as she was.

Loretta is to learn housework and have a little garden of
her own, and particularly play out of doors in the sunshine. She is to go to bed early and be fed up on nice
nourishing food, and they are to pet her and make her
happy. All this for three dollars a week!

Why not find a hundred such families, and board out all
the children? Then this building could be turned into an
idiot-asylum, and I, not knowing anything about idiots,
could conscientiously resign and go back home and live
happily ever after.

Really, Judy, I am growing frightened. This asylum will
get me if I stay long enough. I am becoming so interested
in it that I can't think or talk or dream of anything else.
You and Jervis have blasted all my prospects in life.

Suppose I should retire and marry and have a family; as
families go nowadays, I couldn't hope for more than five
or six children at the most, and all with the same heredity. But, mercy! such a family appears perfectly insignificant and monotonous. You have institutionalized me.

Reproachfully yours,
SALLIE MCBRIDE.

P.S. We have a child here whose father was lynched. Isn't
that a piquant detail to have in one's history?

Dearest Judy:

What shall we do? Mamie Prout does not like prunes. This antipathy to a cheap and healthful foodstuff is nothing but imagination, and ought not to be countenanced among the inmates of a well-managed institution. Mamie must be made to like prunes. So says our grammar teacher, who spends the noonday hour with us and overlooks the morals of our charges. About one o'clock to-day she marched Mamie to my office charged with the offense of refusing, *absolutely* refusing, to open her mouth and put in a prune. The child was plumped down on a stool to await punishment from me.

Now, as you know, I do not like bananas, and I should hate awfully to be forced to swallow them; so, by the same token, why should I force Mamie Prout to swallow prunes?

While I was pondering a course that would seem to uphold Miss Keller's authority, but would at the same time leave a loophole for Mamie, I was called to the telephone.

"Sit there until I come back," I said, and went out and closed the door.

The message was from a kind lady wishing to motor me to a committee meeting. I didn't tell you that I am organizing local interest in our behalf. The idle rich who possess estates in this neighborhood are beginning to drift out from town, and I am laying my plans to catch them before they are deflected by too many garden parties and tennis tournaments. They have never been of the slightest use to this asylum, and I think it's about time they woke up to a realization of our presence.

129

Returning at tea-time, I was waylaid in the hall by Dr. MacRae, who demanded some statistics from my office. I opened the door, and there sat Mamie Prout exactly where she had been left four hours before.

"Mamie darling!" I cried in horror. "You haven't been here all this time?"

"Yes, ma'am," said Mamie; "you told me to wait until you came back."

That poor patient little thing was fairly swaying with weariness, but she never uttered a whimper.

I will say for Sandy that he was *sweet.* He gathered her up in his arms and carried her to my library, and petted her and caressed her back to smiles. Jane brought the sewing-table and spread it before the fire, and while the doctor and I had tea, Mamie had her supper. I suppose, according to the theory of some educators, now, when she was thoroughly worn out and hungry, would have been the psychological moment to ply her with prunes. But you will be pleased to hear that I did nothing of the sort, and that the doctor for once upheld my unscientific principles. Mamie had the most wonderful supper of her life, embellished with strawberry jam from my private jar and peppermints from Sandy's pocket. We returned her to her mates happy and comforted, but still possessing that regrettable distaste for prunes.

Did you ever know anything more appalling than this soul-crushing unreasoning obedience which Mrs. Lippett so insistently fostered? It's the orphan-asylum attitude toward life, and somehow I must crush it out. Initiative, responsibility, curiosity, inventiveness, fight—oh dear! I wish the doctor had a serum for injecting all these useful virtues into an orphan's circulation.

Portrait of an

Obedient Child

LATER.

I wish you'd come back to New York. I've appointed you press-agent for this institution, and we need some of your floweriest writing immediately. There are seven tots here crying to be adopted, and it's your business to adver- tise them.

Little Gertrude is cross-eyed, but dear and affectionate and generous. Can't you write her up so persuasively that some loving family will be willing to take her even if she isn't beautiful? Her eyes can be operated on when she's older; but if it were a cross disposition she had, no surgeon in the world could remove that. The child knows there is something missing, though she has never seen a live parent in her life. She holds up her arms persuasively to every person who passes. Put in all the pathos you are capable of, and see if you can't fetch her a mother and father.

Maybe you can get one of the New York papers to run a Sunday-feature article about a lot of different children. I'll send some photographs. You remember what a lot of responses that "Smiling Joe" picture brought for the Sea Breeze people? I can furnish equally taking portraits of Laughing Lou and Gurgling Gertrude and Kicking Karl if you will just add the literary touch.

And do find me some sports who are not afraid of heredity. This wanting every child to come from one of the first families of Virginia is getting tiresome.

Yours, as usual,
SALLIE.

Friday.

My dear, dear Judy:

Such an upheaval! I've discharged the cook and the housekeeper, and in delicate language conveyed the impression to our grammar teacher that she needn't come back next year. But, oh, if I could only discharge the Honorable Cy!

I must tell you what happened this morning. Our trustee, who has had a dangerous illness, is now dangerously well again, and dropped in to pay a neighborly call. Punch was occupying a rug on my library floor, virtuously engaged with building-blocks. I am separating him from the other kindergarten children, and trying the Montessori method of a private rug and no nervous distraction. I was flattering myself that it was working well; his vocabulary of late has become almost prudish.

After half an hour's desultory visit, the Hon. Cy rose to go. As the door closed behind him (I am at least thankful the child waited for that), Punch raised his appealing brown eyes to mine and murmured, with a confiding smile:

"Gee! ain't he got de hell of a mug?"

If you know a kind Christian family where I can place out a sweet little five-year boy, please communicate at once with

S. McBride,
Sup't John Grier Home.

133

Dear Pendletons:

I've never known anything like you two snails. You've only just reached Washington, and I have had my suit-case packed for days, ready to spend a rejuvenating week-end *chez vous.* Please hurry! I've languished in this asylum atmosphere as long as is humanly possible. I shall gasp and die if I don't get a change.

Yours,

on the point of suffocation,
S. McB.

P.S. Drop a card to Gordon Hallock, telling him you are there. He will be charmed to put himself and the Capitol at your disposal. I know that Jervis doesn't like him, but Jervis ought to get over his baseless prejudices against politicians. Who knows? I may be entering politics myself some day.

My dear Judy:

We do receive the most amazing presents from our friends and benefactors. Listen to this. Last week Mr. Wilton J. Leverett (I quote from his card) ran over a broken bottle outside our gate, and came in to visit the institution while his chauffeur was mending the tire. Betsy showed him about. He took an intelligent interest in everything he saw, particularly our new camps. That is an exhibit which appeals to men. He ended by removing his coat, and playing base-ball with two tribes of Indians. After an hour and a half he suddenly looked at his watch, begged for a glass of water, and bowed himself off.

We had entirely forgotten the episode until this afternoon, when the expressman drove up to the door with a present for the John Grier Home from the chemical laboratories of Wilton J. Leverett. It was a barrel—well, anyway, a good sized keg—full of liquid green soap!

Did I tell you that the seeds for our garden came from Washington? A polite present from Gordon Hallock and the U. S. Government. As an example of what the past régime did not accomplish, Martin Schladerwitz, who has spent three years on this pseudo-farm, knew no more than to dig a grave two feet deep and bury his lettuce seeds!

Oh, you can't imagine the number of fields in which we need making over; but of course you, of all people, can imagine. Little by little I am getting my eyes wide open, and things that just looked funny to me at first, now—oh dear! It's very disillusionizing. Every funny thing that comes up seems to have a little tragedy wrapped inside it.

Just at present we are paying anxious attention to our manners—not orphan-asylum manners, but dancing-school

Dancing School Manners

manners. There is to be nothing Uriah Heepish about our attitude toward the world. The little girls make courtesies when they shake hands, and the boys remove caps and rise when a lady stands, and push in chairs at the table. (Tommy Woolsey shot Sadie Kate into her soup yesterday, to the glee of all observers except Sadie, who is an independent young damsel and doesn't care for these useless masculine attentions.) At first the boys were inclined to jeer, but after observing the politeness of their hero, Percy de Forest Witherspoon, they have come up to the mark like little gentlemen.

Punch is paying a call this morning. For the last half-hour, while I have been busily scratching away to you, he has been established in the window-seat, quietly and undestructively engaged with colored pencils. Betsy, *en passant*, just dropped a kiss upon his nose.

"Aw, gwan!" said Punch, blushing quite pink, and wiping off the caress with a fine show of masculine indifference. But I notice he has resumed work upon his red-and-green landscape with heightened ardor and an attempt at whistling. We'll succeed yet in conquering that young man's temper.

Tuesday.

The doctor is in a very grumbly mood to-day. He called just as the children were marching in to dinner, whereupon he marched, too, and sampled their food, and, oh, my dear! the potatoes were scorched! And such a clishmaclave as that man made! It is the first time the potatoes ever have been scorched, and you know that scorching sometimes happens in the best of families. But you would think from Sandy's language that the cook had scorched them on purpose, in accordance with my orders.

As I have told you before I could do very nicely without Sandy.

Wednesday.

Yesterday being a wonderful sunny day, Betsy and I turned our backs upon duty and motored to the very fancy home of some friends of hers, where we had tea in an Italian garden. Punch and Sadie Kate had been *such* good children all day that at the last moment we telephoned for permission to include them, too.

"Yes, indeed, do bring the little dears," was the enthusiastic response.

But the choice of Punch and Sadie Kate was a mistake.
We ought to have taken Mamie Prout, who has demon-

strated her ability to sit. I shall spare you the details of our
visit; the climax was reached when Punch went gold-
fishing in the bottom of the swimming-pool. Our host

pulled him out by an agitated leg, and the child returned to the asylum swathed in that gentleman's rose-colored bath-robe.

What do you think? Dr. Robin MacRae, in a contrite mood for having been so intensely disagreeable yesterday, has just invited Betsy and me to take supper in his olive-green house next Sunday evening at seven o'clock in order to look at some microscopic slides. The entertainment, I believe, is to consist of a scarlet-fever culture, some alcoholic tissue, and a tubercular gland. These social attentions bore him excessively; but he realizes that if he is to have free scope in applying his theories to the institution he must be a little polite to its superintendent.

I have just read this letter over, and I must admit that it skips lightly from topic to topic. But though it may not contain news of any great moment, I trust you will realize that its writing has consumed every vacant minute during the last three days.

> I am,
>> Most fully occupied,
>> SALLIE MCBRIDE.

P.S. A blessed woman came this morning and said she would take a child for the summer—one of the sickest, weakest, neediest babies I could give her. She had just lost her husband, and wanted something *hard* to do. Isn't that really very touching?

Dear Judy and Jervis:

Brother Jimmie (we are very alliterative!), spurred on by sundry begging letters from me, has at last sent us a present; but he picked it out himself.

We have a monkey! His name is Java.

The children no longer hear the school-bell ring. On the day the creature came, this entire institution formed in line and filed past and shook his paw. Poor Sing's nose is out of joint. I have to *pay* to have him washed.

Sadie Kate is developing into my private secretary. I have her answer the thank-you letters for the institution, and her literary style is making a hit among our benefactors. She invariably calls out a second gift. I had hitherto believed that the Kilcoyne family sprang from the wild west of Ireland, but I begin to suspect that their source was nearer Blarney Castle. You can see from the enclosed copy of the letter she sent to Jimmie what a persuasive pen the young person has. I trust that, in this case at least, it will not bear the fruit that she suggests.

Dear Mr. Jimie:

We thank you very much for the lovly monkey you give. We name him java because that's a warm iland across the ocian where he was born up in a nest like a bird only big the doctor told us.

The first day he come every boy and girl shook his hand and said good morning java his hand feels funny he holds so tite. I was afraid to touch him but now I let him sit on my shoulder and put his arms around my kneck if he wants to. He makes a funny noise that sounds like swering and gets mad when his tale is puled.

We love him dearly and we love you two.

The next time you have to give a present, please send an elifant. Well I guess Ill stop.

Yours truly
SADIE KATE KILCOYNE.

Percy de Forest Witherspoon is still faithful to his little followers, though I am so afraid he will get tired that I urge him to take frequent vacations. He has not only been faithful himself, but has brought in recruits. He has large social connections in the neighborhood, and last Saturday evening he introduced two friends, nice men who sat around the camp-fire and swapped hunting-stories.

One of them was just back from around the world, and told hair-raising anecdotes of the head-hunters of Sarawak, a narrow pink country on the top of Borneo. My little braves pant to grow up and get to Sarawak, and go out on the war-path after head-hunters. Every encyclopedia in this institution has been consulted, and there isn't a boy here who cannot tell you the history, manners, climate, flora, and fungi of Borneo. I only wish Mr. Witherspoon would introduce friends who had been head-hunting in England, France, and Germany, countries not quite so *chic* as Sarawak, but more useful for general culture.

We have a new cook, the fourth since my reign began. I haven't bothered you with my cooking troubles, but institutions don't escape any more than families. The last is a negro woman, a big, fat, smiling, chocolate-colored creature from Souf Ca'lina. And ever since she came on honey dew we've fed! Her name is—what do you guess? *Sallie,* if you please. I suggested that she change it.

"Sho, Miss, I's had dat name Sallie longer 'n you, an' I couldn't get used nohow to answerin' up pert-like when you sings out 'Mollie!' Seems like Sallie jest b'longs to me."

So "Sallie" she remains; but at least there is no danger of our getting our letters mixed, for her last name is nothing so plebeian as McBride. It's Washington-Johnston, with a hyphen.

Sunday.

Our favorite game of late is finding pet names for
Sandy. His austere presence lends itself to caricature. We
have just originated a new batch. The "Laird o' Cockpen"
is Percy's choice.

> The Laird o' Cockpen he's proud and he's great;
>   His mind is ta'en up wi' the things of the state.

Miss Snaith disgustedly calls him "that man," and Betsy
refers to him (in his absence) as "Dr. Cod-Liver." My
present favorite is "Macphairson Clon Glocketty Angus
McClan." But for real poetic feeling, Sadie Kate beats us
all. She calls him "Mister Someday Soon." I don't believe
that the doctor ever dropped into verse but once in his
life, but every child in this institution knows that one
poem by heart.

> Someday soon something nice is going to happen;
>   Be a good little girl and take this hint:
> Swallow with a smile your cod-liver ile,
>   And the first thing you know you will have a peppermint.

It's this evening that Betsy and I attend his supper-party,
and I confess that we are looking forward to seeing the
interior of his gloomy mansion with gleeful eagerness. He
never talks about himself or his past or anybody connected
with himself. He appears to be an isolated figure standing
on a pedestal labeled SCIENCE, without a glimmer of
any ordinary affections or emotions or human frailties
except temper. Betsy and I are simply eaten up with
curiosity to know what sort of past he came out of; but just

let us get inside his house, and to our detective senses it
will tell its own story. So long as the portal was guarded by
a fierce McGurk, we had despaired of ever effecting an
entrance; but now, behold! The door has opened of its
own accord.

To be continued.
S. McB.

Monday.

Dear Judy:

We attended the doctor's supper-party last night, Betsy and Mr. Witherspoon and I. It turned out a passably cheerful occasion, though I will say that it began under heavy auspices.

His house on the inside is all that the outside promises; never in my life have I seen such an interior as that man's dining-room. The walls and carpets and lambrequins are a heavy dark green. A black-marble mantelpiece shelters a few smoking black coals. The furniture is as nearly black as furniture comes. The decorations are two steel engravings in shiny black frames—the "Monarch of the Glen," and the "Stag at Bay."

We tried hard to be light and sparkling, but it was like eating supper in the family vault. Mrs. McGurk, in black alpaca with a black silk apron, clumped around the table, passing cold, heavy things to eat, with a step so firm that she rattled the silver in the sideboard drawers. Her nose was up, and her mouth was down. She clearly does not approve of the master's entertaining, and she wishes to discourage all guests from ever accepting again.

Sandy sort of dimly knows that there is something the matter with his house, and in order to brighten it up a bit in honor of his guests, he had purchased flowers,—dozens of them,—the most exquisite pink Killarney roses and red and yellow tulips. The McGurk had wedged them all together as tight as they would fit into a peacock-blue jardinière, and plumped it down in the center of the table. The thing was as big as a bushel-basket. Betsy and I nearly

145

forgot our manners when we saw that centerpiece; but the doctor seemed so innocently pleased at having obtained a bright note in his dining-room that we suppressed our amusement and complimented him warmly upon his happy color scheme.

The moment supper was over, we hastened with relief to his own part of the house, where the McGurk's influence does not penetrate. No one in a cleaning capacity ever enters either his library or office or laboratory except Llewelyn, a short, wiry, bow-legged Welshman, who combines to a unique degree the qualities of chambermaid and chauffeur.

The library, though not the most cheerful room I have ever seen, still, for a man's house, is not so bad—books all around from floor to ceiling, with the overflow in piles on floor and table and mantelpiece; half a dozen abysmal leather chairs and a rug or so, with another black marble mantelpiece, but this time containing a crackling wood fire. By way of bric-à-brac, he has a stuffed pelican and a crane with a frog in its mouth, also a racoon sitting on a log, and a varnished tarpon. A faint suggestion of iodoform floats in the air.

The doctor made the coffee himself in a French machine, and we dismissed his housekeeper from our spirits. He really did do his best to be a thoughtful host and I have to report that the word "insanity" was not once mentioned. It seems that Sandy, in his moments of relaxation, is a fisherman; he and Percy began swapping stories of salmon and trout, and he finally got out his case of fishing-flies, and gallantly presented Betsy and me with a "silver doctor" and a "Jack Scott" out of which to make hat-pins. Then the conversation wandered to sport on the

Scotch moors, and he told about one time when he was lost, and spent the night out in the heather. There is no doubt about it, Sandy's heart is in the highlands.

I am afraid that Betsy and I have wronged him. Though it is hard to relinquish the interesting idea, he may not, after all, have committed a crime. We are now leaning to the belief that he was crossed in love.

It's really horrid of me to make fun of poor Sandy, for, despite his stern bleakness of disposition, he's a pathetic figure of a man. Think of coming home after an anxious day's round to eat a solitary dinner in that grim dining-room!

Do you suppose it would cheer him up a little if I should send my company of artists to paint a frieze of rabbits around the wall?

With love, as usual,
SALLIE.

Dear Judy:

Aren't you ever coming back to New York? Please hurry! I need a new hat, and am desirous of shopping for it on Fifth Avenue, not on Water Street. Mrs. Gruby, our best milliner, does not believe in slavishly following Paris fashions; she originates her own styles. But three years ago, as a great concession to convention, she did make a tour of the New York shops, and is still creating models on the uplift of that visit.

Also, besides my own hat, I must buy 113 hats for my children, to say nothing of shoes and knickerbockers and shirts and hair-ribbons and stockings and garters. It's quite a task to keep a little family like mine decently clothed.

Did you get that bit letter I wrote you last week? You never had the grace to mention it in yours of Thursday, and it was seventeen pages long, and took me *days* to write.

Yours truly,
S. McBride.

P.S. Why don't you tell me some news about Gordon? Have you seen him, and did he mention me? Is he running after any of those pretty Southern girls that Washington is so full of? You know that I want to hear. Why must you be so beastly uncommunicative?

Tuesday, 4:27 P.M.

Dear Judy:

Your telegram came two minutes ago by telephone.

Yes, thank you, I shall be delighted to arrive at 5:49 on Thursday afternoon. And don't make any engagements for that evening, please, as I intend to sit up until midnight talking John Grier gossip with you and the president.

Friday and Saturday and Monday I shall have to devote to shopping. Oh, yes, you're right; I already possess more clothes than any jail-bird needs, but when spring comes, I *must* have new plumage. As it is, I wear an evening gown every night just to wear them out—no, not entirely that; to make myself believe that I'm still an ordinary girl despite this extraordinary life that you have pushed me into.

The Hon. Cy found me yesterday arrayed in a Nile-green crape (Jane's creation, though it looked Parisian). He was quite puzzled when he found I wasn't going to a ball. I invited him to stay and dine with me, and he accepted! We got on very affably. He expands over his dinner. Food appears to agree with him. If there's any Bernard Shaw in New York just now, I believe that I might spare a couple of hours Saturday afternoon for a matinée. G. B. S.'s dialogue would afford such a life-giving contrast to the Hon. Cy's.

There's no use writing any more; I'll wait and talk.

Addio.
SALLIE.

P.S. Oh dear! just as I had begun to catch glimmerings of niceness in Sandy, he broke out again and was *abominable.*

We unfortunately have five cases of measles in this institution, and the man's manner suggests that Miss Snaith and I gave the measles to the children on purpose to make him trouble. There are many days when I should be willing to accept our doctor's resignation.

Dear Enemy:

Your brief and dignified note of yesterday is at hand. I have never known anybody whose literary style resembled so exactly his spoken word.

And you will be greatly obliged if I will drop my absurd fashion of calling you "Enemy"? I will drop my absurd fashion of calling you Enemy just as soon as you drop your absurd fashion of getting angry and abusive and insulting the moment any little thing goes wrong.

I am leaving to-morrow afternoon to spend four days in New York.

Yours truly,
S. MCBRIDE.

Chez THE PENDLETONS, New York.

My dear Enemy:

I trust that this note will find you in a more affable frame of mind than when I saw you last. I emphatically repeat that it was not due to the carelessness of the superintendent of our institution that those two new cases of measles crept in, but rather to the unfortunate anatomy of our old-fashioned building, which does not permit of the proper isolation of contagious cases.

As you did not deign to visit us yesterday morning before I left, I could not offer any parting suggestions. I therefore write to ask that you cast your critical eye upon Mamie Prout. She is covered all over with little red spots which may be measles, though I am hoping not. Mamie spots very easily.

I return to prison life next Monday at six o'clock.

Yours truly,
S. McBride.

P.S. I trust you will pardon my mentioning it, but you are not the kind of doctor that I admire. I like them chubby and round and smiling.

THE JOHN GRIER HOME,
June 9.

Dear Judy:

You are an awful family for an impressionable young girl
to visit. How can you expect me to come back and settle
down contentedly to institution life after witnessing such a
happy picture of domestic concord as the Pendleton household presents?

All the way back in the train, instead of occupying
myself with the two novels, four magazines, and one box
of chocolates that your husband thoughtfully provided, I
spent the time in a mental review of the young men of my
acquaintance to see if I couldn't discover one as nice as
Jervis. I did! (A little nicer, I think.) From this day on he
is the marked-down victim, the destined prey.

I shall hate to give up the asylum after getting so
excited over it, but unless you are willing to move it to
the capital, I don't see any alternative.

The train was awfully late. We sat and smoked on a
siding while two accommodations and a freight dashed
past. I think we must have broken something, and had to
tinker up our engine. The conductor was soothing, but
uncommunicative.

It was 7:30 when I descended, the only passenger, at
our insignificant station in the pitch darkness and *rain*,
without an umbrella, and wearing that precious new hat.
No Turnfelt to meet me; not even a station hack. To be
sure, I hadn't telegraphed the exact time of my arrival,
but, still, I did feel rather neglected. I had sort of vaguely
expected all *one hundred and thirteen* to be drawn up by the

platform, scattering flowers and singing songs of welcome.
Just as I was telling the station man that I would watch his
telegraph instrument while he ran across to the corner
saloon and telephoned for a vehicle, there came whirling
around the corner two big search-lights aimed straight at
me. They stopped nine inches before running me down,
and I heard Sandy's voice saying:

"Weel, weel, Miss Sallie McBride! I'm thinking it's ower
time you came back to tak' the bit bairns off my hands."

That man had come three times to meet me on the off
chance of the train's getting in some time. He tucked me
and my new hat and bags and books and chocolates all in
under his waterproof flap, and we splashed off. Really, I
felt as if I was getting back home again, and quite sad at
the thought of ever having to leave. Mentally, you see, I
had already resigned and packed and gone. The mere idea
that you are not in a place for the rest of your life gives
you an awfully unstable feeling. That's why trial marriages
would never work. You've got to feel you're in a thing
irrevocably and forever in order to buckle down and really
put your whole mind into making it a success.

It's astounding how much news can accrue in four days.
Sandy just couldn't talk fast enough to tell me everything
I wanted to hear. Among other items, I learned that Sadie
Kate had spent two days in the infirmary, her malady
being, according to the doctor's diagnosis, half a jar of
gooseberry jam and Heaven knows how many doughnuts.
Her work had been changed during my absence to dish-
washing in the officers' pantry, and the juxtaposition of so
many exotic luxuries was too much for her fragile virtue.

Also, our colored cook Sallie and our colored useful
man Noah have entered upon a war of extermination.

The original trouble was over a little matter of kindling, augmented by a pail of hot water that Sallie threw out of the window with, for a woman, unusual accuracy of aim. You can see what a rare character the head of an orphan-asylum must have. She has to combine the qualities of a baby nurse and a police magistrate.

The doctor had told only the half when we reached the house, and as he had not yet dined, owing to meeting me three times, I begged him to accept the hospitality of the John Grier. I would get Betsy and Mr. Witherspoon, and we would hold an executive meeting, and settle all our neglected businesses.

Sandy accepted with flattering promptness. He likes to dine outside of the family vault.

But Betsy, I found, had dashed home to greet a visiting grandparent, and Percy was playing bridge in the village. It's seldom the young thing gets out of an evening, and I'm glad for him to have a little cheerful diversion.

So it ended in the doctor's and my dining tête-à-tête on a hastily improvised dinner,—it was then close upon eight, and our normal dinner hour is 6:30,—but it was such an improvised dinner as I am sure Mrs. McGurk never served him. Sallie, wishing to impress me with her invaluableness, did her absolutely Southern best. And after dinner we had coffee before the fire in my comfortable blue library, while the wind howled outside and the shutters banged.

We passed a most cordial and intimate evening. For the first time since our acquaintance I struck a new note in the man. There really is something attractive about him when you once come to know him. But the process of knowing him requires time and tact. He's no' very gleg at

the uptak. I've never seen such a tantalizingly inexplicable
person. All the time I'm talking to him I feel as though
behind his straight line of a mouth and his half-shut eyes
there were banked fires smoldering inside. Are you sure
he hasn't committed a crime? He does manage to convey
the delicious feeling that he has.

And I must add that Sandy's not so bad a talker when
he lets himself go. He has the entire volume of Scotch
literature at his tongue's end.

"Little kens the auld wife as she sits by the fire what the
wind is doing on Hurly-Burly-Swire," he observed as a
specially fierce blast drove the rain against the window. That
sounds pat, doesn't it? I haven't, though, the remotest idea
what it means. And listen to this: between cups of coffee
(he drinks far too much coffee for a sensible medical man)
he casually let fall the news that his family knew the R. L. S.
family personally, and used to take supper at 17 Heriot Row!
I tended him assiduously for the rest of the evening in a

> Did you once see Shelley plain,
> And did he stop and speak to you?

frame of mind.

When I started this letter, I had no intention of filling it
with a description of the recently excavated Charms of
Robin MacRae; it's just by way of remorseful apology. He
was so nice and companionable last night that I have been
going about to-day feeling conscience-smitten at the thought
of how mercilessly I made fun of him to you and Jervis. I
really didn't mean quite all of the impolite things that I
said. About once a month the man is sweet and tractable
and engaging.

Punch has just been paying a social call, and during the course of it he lost three little toadlings an inch long. Sadie Kate recovered one of them from under the bookcase, but the other two hopped away; and I'm so afraid they've taken sanctuary in my bed! I do wish that mice and snakes and toads and angleworms were not so portable. You never know what is going on in a perfectly respectable-looking child's pocket.

I had a beautiful visit in Casa Pendleton. Don't forget your promise to return it soon.

Yours as ever,
SALLIE.

P.S. I left a pair of pale-blue bedroom slippers under the bed. Will you please have Mary wrap them up and mail them to me? And hold her hand while she writes the address. She spelt my name on the place cards "Mackbird."

Dear Enemy:

As I told you, I left an application for an accomplished nurse with the employment bureau of New York.

Wanted! A nurse maid with an ample lap suitable for the accommodation of seventeen babies at once.

She came this afternoon, and this is the fine figure of a woman that I drew!

We couldn't keep a baby from sliding off her lap unless we fastened him firmly with safety-pins.

Please give Sadie Kate the magazine. I'll read it to-night and return it to-morrow.

Was there ever a more docile and obedient pupil than
S. McBride?

My dear Judy:

I've been spending the last three days busily getting under way all those latest innovations that we planned in New York. Your word is law. A public cooky-jar has been established.

Also, the eighty play-boxes have been ordered. It is a wonderful idea, having a private box for each child, where he can store up his treasures. The ownership of a little personal property will help develop them into responsible citizens. I ought to have thought of it myself, but for some reason the idea didn't come. Poor Judy! You have inside knowledge of the longings of their little hearts that I shall never be able to achieve, not with all the sympathy I can muster.

We are doing our best to run this institution with as few discommoding rules as possible, but in regard to those play-boxes there is one point on which I shall have to be firm. The children may not keep in them mice or toads or angleworms.

I can't tell you how pleased I am that Betsy's salary is to be raised, and that we are to keep her permanently. But the Hon. Cy Wykoff deprecates the step. He has been making inquiries, and he finds that her people are perfectly able to take care of her without any salary.

"You don't furnish legal advice for nothing," say I to him. "Why should she furnish her trained services for nothing?"

"This is charitable work."

"Then work which is undertaken for your own good

should be paid, but work which is undertaken for the public good should not be paid?"

"Fiddlesticks!" says he. "She's a woman, and her family ought to support her."

This opened up vistas of argument which I did not care to enter with the Hon. Cy, so I asked him whether he thought it would be nicer to have a real lawn or hay on the slope that leads to the gate. He likes to be consulted, and I pamper him as much as possible in all unessential details. You see, I am following Sandy's canny advice: "Trustees are like fiddle-strings; they maunna be screwed ower tight. Humor the mon, but gang your ain gait." Oh, the tact that this asylum is teaching me! I should make a wonderful politician's wife.

Thursday night.

You will be interested to hear that I have temporarily placed out Punch with two charming spinsters who have long been tottering on the brink of a child. They finally came last week, and said they would like to try one for a month to see what the sensation felt like.

They wanted, of course, a pretty ornament, dressed in pink and white and descended from the *Mayflower*. I told them that any one could bring up a daughter of the *Mayflower* to be an ornament to society, but the real feat was to bring up a son of an Italian organ-grinder and an Irish washerwoman. And I offered Punch. That Neapolitan heredity of his, artistically speaking, may turn out a glorious mixture, if the right environment comes along to choke out all the weeds.

I put it up to them as a sporting proposition, and they

were game. They have agreed to take him for one month and concentrate upon his remaking all their years of conserved force, to the end that he may be fit for adoption in some moral family. They both have a sense of humor and *accomplishing* characters, or I should never have dared to propose it. And really I believe it's going to be the one way of taming our young fire-eater. They will furnish the affection and caresses and attention that in his whole abused little life he has never had.

They live in a fascinating old house with an Italian garden, and furnishings selected from the whole round world. It does seem like sacrilege to turn that destructive child loose in such a collection of treasures. But he hasn't broken anything here for more than a month, and I believe that the Italian in him will respond to all that beauty.

I warned them that they must not shrink from any profanity that might issue from his pretty baby lips.

He departed last night in a very fancy automobile, and maybe I wasn't glad to say good-by to our disreputable young man! He has absorbed just about half of my energy.

Friday.

The pendant arrived this morning. Many thanks! But you really ought not to have given me another; a hostess cannot be held accountable for all the things that careless guests lose in her house. It is far too pretty for my chain. I am thinking of having my nose pierced, Cingalese fashion, and wearing my new jewel where it will really show.

I must tell you that our Percy is putting some good constructive work into this asylum. He has founded the

John Grier Bank, and has worked out all the details in a very professional and businesslike fashion, entirely incomprehensible to my non-mathematical mind. All of the older children possess properly printed checkbooks, and they are each to be paid five dollars a week for their services, such as going to school and accomplishing housework. They are then to pay the institution (by check) for their board and clothes, which will consume their five dollars. It looks like a vicious circle, but it's really very educative; they will comprehend the value of money before we dump them into a mercenary world. Those who are particularly good in lessons or work will receive an extra recompense. My head aches at the thought of the bookkeeping, but Percy waves that aside as a mere bagatelle. It is to be accomplished by our prize arithmeticians, and will train them for positions of trust. If Jervis hears of any opening for bank officials, let me know; I shall have a well-trained president, cashier, and paying-teller ready to be placed by this time next year.

Saturday.

Our doctor doesn't like to be called "Enemy." It hurts his feelings or his dignity or something of the sort; but since I will persist, despite his expostulations, he has finally retaliated with a nickname for me. He calls me "Miss Sally Lunn," and is in a glow of pride at having achieved such an imaginative flight.

He and I have invented a new pastime: he talks Scotch, and I answer in Irish. Our conversations run like this:

"Good afthernoon to ye, docther. An' how's yer health the day?"

"Verra weel, verra weel. And how gaes it wi' a' the bairns?"

"Shure, they're all av thim doin' foin."

"I'm gey glad to hear it. This saft weather is hard on folk. There's muckle sickness aboot the kintra."

"Hiven be praised it has not lighted here! But sit down, docther, an' make yersilf at home. Will ye be afther havin' a cup o' tay?"

"Hoot, woman! I would na hae you fash yoursel', but a wee drap tea winna coom amiss."

"Whist! It's no thruble at all."

You may not think this a very dizzying excursion into frivolity; but I assure you, for one of Sandy's dignity, it's positively riotous. The man has been in a heavenly temper ever since I came back; not a single cross word. I am beginning to think I may reform him as well as Punch.

This letter must be about long enough even for you; I've been writing it bit by bit for three days, whenever I happened to pass my desk.

Yours as ever,
SALLIE.

P.S. I don't think much of your vaunted prescription for hair tonic. Either the druggist didn't mix it right, or Jane didn't apply it with discretion. I stuck to the pillow this morning.

Dear Gordon:

Your letter of Thursday is at hand, and extremely silly I consider it. Of course I am not trying to let you down easy; that isn't my way. If I let you down at all, it will be suddenly and with an awful bump. But I honestly didn't realize that it had been three weeks since I wrote. Please excuse!

Also, my dear sir, I have to bring you to account. You were in New York last week, and you never ran up to see us. You thought we wouldn't find it out, but we heard—and are insulted.

Would you like an outline of my day's activities? Wrote monthly report for trustees' meeting. Audited accounts. Entertained agent of State Charities Aid Association for luncheon. Supervised children's menus for next ten days. Dictated five letters to families who have our children. Visited our little feeble-minded Loretta Higgins (pardon the reference; I know you don't like me to mention the feeble-minded), who is being boarded out in a nice comfortable family, where she is learning to work. Came back to tea and a conference with the doctor about sending a child with tubercular glands to a sanatorium. Read an article on cottage *versus* congregate system for housing dependent children. (We do need cottages! I wish you'd send us a few for a Christmas present.) And now at nine o'clock I'm sleepily beginning a letter to you. Do you know many young society girls who can point to such a useful day as that?

165

Oh, I forgot to say that I stole ten minutes from my accounts this morning to install a new cook. Our Sallie Washington-Johnston, who cooked fit for the angels, had a dreadful, dreadful temper and terrorized poor Noah, our super-excellent furnace-man, to the point of giving notice. We couldn't spare Noah. He's more useful to the institution than its superintendent, and so Sallie Washington-Johnston is no more.

When I asked the new cook her name, she replied, "Ma name is Suzanne Estelle, but ma friends call me Pet." Pet cooked the dinner to-night, but I must say that she lacks Sallie's delicate touch. I am awfully disappointed that you didn't visit us while Sallie was still here. You would have taken away an exalted opinion of my housekeeping.

Drowsiness overcame me at that point, and it's now two days later.

Poor neglected Gordon! It has just occurred to me that you never got thanked for the modeling-clay which came two weeks ago, and it was such an unusually intelligent present that I should have telegraphed my appreciation. When I opened the box and saw all that nice messy putty stuff, I sat down on the spot and created a statue of Singapore. The children love it; and it is very good to have the handicraft side of their training encouraged.

After a careful study of American history, I have determined that nothing is so valuable to a future president as an early obligatory unescapable performance of *chores*.

Therefore I have divided the daily work of this institution into a hundred parcels, and the children rotate weekly through a succession of unaccustomed tasks. Of course they do everything badly, for just as they learn how, they progress to something new. It would be infinitely easier for us to follow Mrs. Lippett's immoral custom of keeping each child sentenced for life to a well-learned routine; but when the temptation assails me, I recall the dreary picture of Florence Henty, who polished the brass door-knobs of this institution for seven years—and I sternly shove the children on.

I get angry every time I think of Mrs. Lippett. She had exactly the point of view of a Tammany politician—no slightest sense of service to society; her only interest in the John Grier Home was to get a living out of it.

Wednesday.

What new branch of learning do you think I have introduced into my asylum? Table manners!

I never had any idea that it was such a lot of trouble to teach children how to eat and drink. Their favorite method is to put their mouths down to their mugs and lap their milk like kittens. Good manners are not merely snobbish ornaments, as Mrs. Lippett's régime appeared to believe; they mean self-discipline and thought for others, and my children have got to learn them.

That woman never allowed them to talk at their meals, and I am having the most dreadful time getting any conversation out of them above a frightened whisper. So I have instituted the custom of the entire staff, myself included, sitting with them at the table, and directing the talk along cheerful and improving lines. Also I have established a small, very strict training-table, where the little dears, in relays, undergo a week of steady badgering. Our uplifting table conversations run like this:

"Yes, Tom, Napoleon Bonaparte was a very great man—elbows off the table. He possessed a tremendous power of concentrating his mind on whatever he wanted to have; and that is the way to accomplish—don't snatch, Susan; ask politely for the bread, and Carrie will pass it to you.—But he was an example of the fact that selfish thought just for oneself, without considering the lives of others, will come to disaster in the—Tom! Keep your mouth shut when you chew—and after the battle of Waterloo—let Sadie's cooky alone—his fall was all the greater because—Sadie Kate, you may leave the table. It makes no difference what he did. Under no provocation does a lady slap a gentleman."

Two more days have passed; this is the same kind of meandering letter I write to Judy. At least, my dear man, you can't complain that I haven't been thinking about you this week! I know you hate to be told all about the asylum, but I can't help it, for it's all I know. I don't have five minutes a day to read the papers. The big outside world has dropped away. My interests all lie on the inside of this little iron inclosure.

I am at present,

S. MCBRIDE,

Superintendent of the

John Grier Home.

Thursday.

Dear Enemy:

"Time is but the stream I go a-fishing in." Hasn't that a very philosophical, detached, Lord of the Universe sound? It comes from Thoreau, whom I am assiduously reading at present. As you see, I have revolted against your literature and taken to my own again. The last two evenings have been devoted to "Walden," a book as far removed as possible from the problems of the dependent child.

Did you ever read old Henry David Thoreau? You really ought; I think you'd find him a congenial soul. Listen to this: "Society is commonly too cheap. We meet at very short intervals, not having had time to acquire any new value for each other. It would be better if there were but one habitation to a square mile, as where I live." A pleasant, expansive, neeborlike man he must have been! He minds me in some ways o' Sandy.

This is to tell you that we have a placing-out agent visiting us. She is about to dispose of four chicks, one of them Thomas Kehoe. What do you think? Ought we to risk it? The place she has in mind for him is a farm in a no-license portion of Connecticut, where he will work hard for his board, and live in the farmer's family. It sounds exactly the right thing, and we can't keep him here forever; he'll have to be turned out some day into a world full of whisky.

I'm sorry to tear you away from that cheerful work on "Dementia Precox," but I'd be most obliged if you'd drop in here toward eight o'clock for a conference with the agent.

I am, as usual,
S. McBride.

My *dear Judy:*

Betsy has perpetrated a most unconscionable trick upon a pair of adopting parents. They have traveled East from Ohio in their touring-car for the dual purpose of seeing the country and picking up a daughter. They appear to be the leading citizens of their town, whose name at the moment escapes me; but it's a very important town. It has electric lights and gas, and Mr. Leading Citizen owns the controlling interest in both plants. With a wave of his hand he could plunge that entire town into darkness; but fortunately he's a kind man, and won't do anything so harsh, not even if they fail to reëlect him mayor. He lives in a brick house with a slate roof and two towers, and has a deer and fountain and lots of nice shade-trees in the yard. (He carries its photograph in his pocket.) They are good-natured, generous, kind-hearted, smiling people, and a little fat; you can see what desirable parents they would make.

Well, we had exactly the daughter of their dreams, only, as they came without giving us notice, she was dressed in a flannellet nightgown, and her face was dirty. They looked Caroline over, and were not impressed; but they thanked us politely, and said they would bear her in mind. They wanted to visit the New York Orphanage before deciding. We knew well that, if they saw that superior assemblage of children, our poor little Caroline would never have a chance.

Then Betsy rose to the emergency. She graciously in-vited them to motor over to her house for tea that afternoon and inspect one of our little wards who would be visiting her baby niece. Mr. and Mrs. Leading Citizen do not know many people in the East, and they haven't been receiving the invitations that they feel are their due; so they were quite innocently pleased at the prospect of a little social diversion. The moment they had retired to the hotel for luncheon, Betsy called up her car, and rushed baby Caroline over to her house. She stuffed her into baby niece's best pink-and-white embroidered frock, borrowed a hat of Irish lace, some pink socks and white slippers, and set her picturesquely upon the green lawn under a spreading beech-tree. A white-aproned nurse (borrowed also from baby niece) plied her with bread and milk and gaily colored toys. By the time prospective parents arrived, our Caroline, full of food and contentment, greeted them with cooes of delight. From the moment their eyes fell upon her they were ravished with desire. Not a suspicion crossed their unobservant minds that this sweet little rosebud was the child of the morning. And so, a few formalities having been complied with, it really looks as though baby Caroline would live in the Towers and grow into a leading citizen.

I must really get to work, without any further delay, upon the burning question of new clothes for our girls.

With the highest esteem, I am,

D'r Ma'am,

Y'r most ob'd't and h'mble serv't,

SAL. MCBRIDE.

                                                    June 19th.

My *dearest Judy:*
   Listen to the grandest innovation of all, and one that
will delight your heart.

NO MORE BLUE GINGHAM!

   Feeling that this aristocratic neighborhood of country
estates might contain valuable food for our asylum, I
have of late been moving in the village social circles,
and at a luncheon yesterday I dug out a beautiful and
charming widow who wears delectable, flowing gowns
that she designs herself. She confided to me that she
would have loved to have been a dressmaker, if she
had only been born with a needle in her mouth instead
of a golden spoon. She says she never sees a pretty
girl badly dressed but she longs to take her in hand and
make her over. Did you ever hear anything so apropos?
From the moment she opened her lips she was a marked
man.
   "I can show you fifty-nine badly dressed girls," said I to
her, "and you have got to come back with me and plan
their new clothes and make them beautiful."
   She expostulated; but in vain. I led her out to her
automobile, shoved her in, and murmured, "John Grier
Home" to the chauffeur. The first inmate our eyes fell
upon was Sadie Kate, just fresh, I judge, from hugging
the molasses-barrel; and a shocking spectacle she was
for any esthetically minded person. In addition to the
stickiness, one stocking was coming down, her pinafore
was buttoned crookedly, and she had lost a hair-ribbon.

                          172

But—as always—completely at ease, she welcomed us with a cheery grin, and offered the lady a sticky paw.

"Now," said I, in triumph, "you see how much we need you. What can you do to make Sadie Kate beautiful?"

"Wash her," said Mrs. Livermore.

Sadie Kate was marched to my bathroom. When the scrubbing was finished and the hair strained back and the stocking restored to seemly heights, I returned her for a second inspection—a perfectly normal little orphan. Mrs. Livermore turned her from side to side, and studied her long and earnestly.

Sadie Kate by nature is a beauty, a wild, dark, Gipsyish little colleen; she looks fresh from the wind-swept moors of Connemara. But, oh, we have managed to rob her of her birthright with this awful institution uniform!

After five minutes' silent contemplation, Mrs. Livermore raised her eyes to mine.

"Yes, my dear, you need me."

And then and there we formed our plans. She is to head the committee on CLOTHES. She is to choose three friends to help her; and they, with the two dozen best sewers among the girls and our sewing-teacher and five sewing-machines, are going to make over the looks of this institution. And the charity is all on our side. We are supplying Mrs. Livermore with the profession that Providence robbed her of. Wasn't it clever of me to find her? I woke this morning at dawn and crowed!

Lots more news,—I could run into a second volume,—but I am going to send this letter to town by Mr. Witherspoon, who, in a very high collar and the blackest of evening clothes, is on the point of departure for a barn dance at the country club. I told him to pick out the

A Study in Clothes

nicest girls he danced with to come and tell stories to my children.

It is dreadful, the scheming person I am getting to be. All the time I am talking to any one, I am silently thinking, "What use can you be to my asylum?"

There is grave danger that this present superintendent will become so interested in her job that she will never want to leave. I sometimes picture her a white-haired old lady, propelled about the building in a wheeled chair, but still tenaciously superintending her fourth generation of orphans.

Please discharge her before that day!

Yours,
SALLIE.

Dear Judy:

Yesterday morning, without the slightest warning, a station hack drove up to the door and disgorged upon the steps two men, two little boys, a baby girl, a rocking-horse, and a Teddy bear, and then drove off!

The men were artists, and the little ones were children of another artist, dead three weeks ago. They had brought the mites to us because they thought "John Grier" sounded solid and respectable, and not like a public institution. It had never entered their unbusinesslike heads that any formality is necessary about placing a child in an asylum.

I explained that we were full, but they seemed so stranded and aghast, that I told them to sit down while I advised them what to do. So the chicks were sent to the nursery, with a recommendation of bread and milk, while I listened to their history. Those artists had a fatally literary touch, or maybe it was just the sound of the baby girl's laugh, but, anyway, before they had finished, the babes were ours.

Never have I seen a sunnier creature than the little Allegra (we don't often get such fancy names or such fancy children). She is three years old, is lisping funny baby-talk and bubbling with laughter. The tragedy she has just emerged from has never touched her. But Don and Clifford, sturdy little lads of five and seven, are already solemn-eyed and frightened at the hardness of life.

Their mother was a kindergarten teacher who married an artist on a capital of enthusiasm and a few tubes of paint. His friends say that he had talent, but of course he

175

had to throw it away to pay the milkman. They lived in a haphazard fashion in a rickety old studio, cooking behind screens, the babies sleeping on shelves.

But there seems to have been a very happy side to it—a great deal of love and many friends, all more or less poor, but artistic and congenial and high-thinking. The little lads, in their gentleness and fineness, show that phase of their upbringing. They have an air which many of my children, despite all the good manners I can pour into them, will forever lack.

The mother died in the hospital a few days after Allegra's birth, and the father struggled on for two years, caring for his brood and painting like mad—advertisements, anything—to keep a roof over their heads.

He died in St. Vincent's three weeks ago,—overwork, worry, pneumonia. His friends rallied about the babies, sold such of the studio fittings as had escaped pawning, paid off the debts, and looked about for the best asylum they could find. And, Heaven save them! they hit upon us!

Well, I kept the two artists for luncheon,—nice creatures in soft hats and Windsor ties, and looking pretty frayed themselves,—and then started them back to New York with the promise that I would give the little family my most parental attention.

So here they are, one little mite in the nursery, two in the kindergarten-room, four big packing-cases full of canvases in the cellar, and a trunk in the store-room with the letters of their father and mother. And a look in their faces, an intangible spiritual *something*, that is their heritage.

I can't get them out of my mind. All night long I was planning their future. The boys are easy; they have already been graduated from college, Mr. Pendleton assisting, and are pursuing honorable business careers. But Allegra I don't know about; I can't think what to wish for the child. Of course the normal thing to wish for any sweet little girl is that two kind foster-parents will come along to take the place of the real parents that Fate has robbed her of; but in this case it would be cruel to steal her away from her brothers. Their love for the baby is pitiful. You see, they have brought her up. The only time I ever hear them laugh is when she has done something funny. The poor little fellows miss their father horribly. I found Don, the five-year-old one, sobbing in his crib last night because he couldn't say good night to "daddy."

But Allegra is true to her name, the happiest young miss of three I have ever seen. The poor father managed well by her, and she, little ingrate, has already forgotten that she has lost him.

Whatever can I do with these little ones? I think and think and think about them. I can't place them out, and it does seem too awful to bring them up here; for as good as we are going to be when we get ourselves made over, still, after all, we are an institution, and our inmates are just little incubator chicks. They don't get the individual, fussy care that only an old hen can give.

There is a lot of interesting news that I might have been telling you, but my new little family has driven everything out of my mind.

Bairns are certain joy, but nae sma' care.

Yours ever,
SALLIE.

P.S. Don't forget that you are coming to visit me next week.

P.S. II. The doctor, who is ordinarily so scientific and unsentimental, has fallen in love with Allegra. He didn't so much as glance at her tonsils; he simply picked her up in his arms and hugged her. Oh, she is a little witch! Whatever is to become of her?

June 22.

My *dear Judy:*

I may report that you need no longer worry as to our inadequate fire protection. The doctor and Mr. Witherspoon have been giving the matter their gravest attention, and no game yet devised has proved so entertaining and destructive as our fire-drill.

The children all retire to their beds and plunge into alert slumber. Fire-alarm sounds. They spring up and into their shoes, snatch the top blanket from their beds, wrap it around their imaginary night-clothes, fall into line, and trot to the hall and stairs.

Our seventeen little tots in the nursery are each in charge of an Indian, and are bundled out, shrieking with delight. The remaining Indians, so long as there is no danger of the roof falling, devote themselves to salvage. On the occasion of our first drill, Percy in command, the contents of a dozen clothes-lockers were dumped into sheets and hurled out of the windows. I usurped dictatorship just in time to keep the pillows and mattresses from following. We spent hours re-sorting those clothes, while Percy and the doctor, having lost all interest, strolled up to the camp with their pipes.

Our future drills are to be a touch less realistic. However, I am pleased to tell you that, under the able direction of Fire-chief Witherspoon, we emptied the building in six minutes and twenty-eight seconds.

That baby Allegra has fairy blood in her veins. Never did this institution harbor such a child, barring one

that Jervis and I know of. She has completely subju-
gated the doctor. Instead of going about his visits like a
sober medical man, he comes down to my library hand in
hand with Allegra, and for half an hour at a time crawls
about on a rug, pretending he's a horse, while the bonnie
wee lassie sits on his back and kicks.

You know, I am thinking of putting a card in the
paper:

> Characters neatly remodeled.
> S. McBride.

Sandy dropped in two nights ago to have a bit of
conversation with Betsy and me, and he was *frivolous*. He
made three jokes, and he sat down at the piano and sang
some old Scotch, "My luve's like a red, red rose," and
"Come under my plaidie," and "Wha's at the window?
Wha? Wha?" not in the least educational, and then danced
a few steps of the strathspey!

I sat and beamed upon my handiwork, for it's true,
I've done it all through my frivolous example and the
books I've given him and the introducing of such light-
some companions as Jimmie and Percy and Gordon
Hallock. If I have a few more months in which to work,
I shall get the man human. He has given up purple ties,
and at my tactful suggestion has adopted a suit of gray.
You have no idea how it sets him off. He will be quite
distinguished-looking as soon as I can make him stop
carrying bulgy things in his pockets.

Good-by; and remember that we're expecting you on
Friday.

SALLIE.

P.S. Here is a picture of Allegra, taken by Mr. Witherspoon. Isn't she a love? Her present clothes do not enhance her beauty, but in the course of a few weeks she will move into a pink smocked frock.

Wednesday, June 24, 10 A.M.

MRS. JERVIS PENDLETON.

Madam:

Your letter is at hand, stating that you cannot visit me on Friday per promise, because your husband has business that keeps him in town. What clishmaclaver is this! Has it come to such a pass that you can't leave him for two days?

I did not let 113 babies interfere with my visit to you, and I see no reason why you should let one husband interfere with your visit to me. I shall meet the Berkshire express on Friday as agreed.

S. MCBRIDE.

My *dear Judy:*

That was a very flying visit you paid us; but for all small favors we are grateful. I am awfully pleased that you were so delighted with the way things are going, and I can't wait for Jervis and the architect to get up here and really begin a fundamental ripping-up.

You know, I had the queerest feeling all the time that you were here. I can't make it seem true that you, my dear, wonderful Judy, were actually brought up in this institution, and know from the bitter inside what these little tots need. Sometimes the tragedy of your childhood fills me with an anger that makes me want to roll up my sleeves and fight the whole world and force it into making itself over into a place more fit for children to live in. That Scotch-Irish ancestry of mine seems to have deposited a tremendous amount of *fight* in my character.

If you had started me with a modern asylum, equipped with nice, clean, hygienic cottages and everything in running order, I couldn't have stood the monotony of its perfect clockwork. It's the sight of so many things crying to be done that makes it possible for me to stay. Sometimes, I must confess, I wake up in the morning and listen to these institution noises, and sniff this institution air, and long for the happy, care-free life that by rights is mine.

You, my dear witch, cast a spell over me, and I came; but often in the night watches your spell wears thin, and I start the day with the burning decision to run away from ths John Grier Home. But I postpone starting until after

breakfast. And as I issue into the corridor, one of these
pathetic tots runs to meet me, and shyly slips a warm,
crumpled little fist into my hand, and looks up with wide
baby eyes, mutely asking for a little petting, and I snatch
him up and hug him; and then, as I look over his shoulder
at the other forlorn little mites, I long to take all 113 into
my arms and love them into happiness. There is something hypnotic about this working with children. Struggle
as you may, it gets you in the end.

Your visit seems to have left me in a broadly philosophical frame of mind; but I really have one or two bits of
news that I might convey. The new frocks are marching
along, and, oh, but they are going to be sweet! Mrs.
Livermore was entranced with those parti-colored bales of
cotton cloth you sent,—you should see our workroom,
with it all scattered about,—and when I think of sixty
little girls, attired in pink and blue and yellow and laven-
der, romping upon our lawn of a sunny day, I feel that we
should have a supply of smoked eye-glasses to offer visitors.
Of course you know that some of those brilliant fabrics are
going to be very fadeable and imprractical; but Mrs. Livermore is as bad as you—she doesn't give a hang. She'll
make a second and a third set if necessary. DOWN WITH
CHECKED GINGHAM!

I am glad you liked our doctor. Of course we reserve the
right to say anything about him we choose, but our feelings would be awfully hurt if anybody else should make fun
of him.

He and I are still superintending each other's reading.
Last week he appeared with Herbert Spencer's "System of
Synthetic Philosophy" for me to glance at; I gratefully
accepted it, and gave him in return the "Diary of Marie

Bashkirtseff." Do you remember in college how we used to enrich our daily speech with quotations from Marie? Well, Sandy took her home and read her painstakingly and thoughtfully.

"Yes," he acknowledged to-day when he came to report, "it is a truthful record of a certain kind of morbid,

egotistical personality that unfortunately does exist; but I can't understand why you care to read it; for, thank God! Sally Lunn, you and Bash haven't anything in common."

That's the nearest to a compliment he ever came, and I feel extremely flattered. As to poor Marie, he refers to her as "Bash" because he can't pronounce her name, and is too disdainful to try.

We have a child here, the daughter of a chorus-girl, and she is a conceited, selfish, vain, posing, morbid, lying little minx, but she has eyelashes! Sandy has taken the most violent dislike to that child; and since reading poor Marie's diary, he has found a new comprehensive adjective for summing up all of her distressing qualities. He calls her *bash*y, and dismisses her.

Good-by and come again.

SALLIE.

P.S. My children show a distressing tendency to draw out their entire bank-accounts to buy candy.

Tuesday night.

My *dear Judy:*

What do you think Sandy has done now? He has gone off on a pleasure-trip to that psychopathic institution whose head alienist visited us a month or so ago. Did you ever know anything like the man? He is fascinated by insane people, and can't let them alone.

When I asked for some parting medical instructions, he replied:

"Feed a cowld and hunger a colic and put nae faith in doctors."

With that advice, and a few bottles of cod-liver oil we are left to our own devices. I feel very free and adventurous. Perhaps you had better run up here again, as there's no telling what joyous upheaval I may accomplish when out from under Sandy's dampening influence.

S.

Dear Enemy:

Here I stay lashed to the mast, while you run about the country disporting yourself with insane people. And just as I was thinking that I had nicely cured you of this morbid predilection for psychopathic institutions! It's very disappointing. You had seemed almost human of late.

May I ask how long you are intending to stay? You had permission to go for two days, and you've already been away four. Charlie Martin fell out of a cherry-tree yesterday and cut his head open, and we were driven to calling in a foreign doctor. Five stitches. Patient doing well. But we don't like to depend on strangers. I wouldn't say a word if you were away on legitimate business, but you know very well that, after associating with melancholics for a week, you will come back home in a dreadful state of gloom, dead-sure that humanity is going to the dogs; and upon me will fall the burden of getting you decently cheerful again.

Do leave those insane people to their delusions, and come back to the John Grier Home, which needs you.

I am most fervent'
Your friend and servant,
S. McB.

P.S. Don't you admire that poetical ending? It was borrowed from Robert Burns, whose works I am reading assiduously as a compliment to a Scotch friend.

July 6.

Dear Judy:

That doctor man is still away. No word; just disappeared
into space. I don't know whether he is ever coming back or
not, but we seem to be running very happily without him.

I lunched yesterday *chez* the two kind ladies who have
taken our Punch to their hearts. The young man seems to be
very much at home. He took me by the hand, and did the
honors of the garden, presenting me with the bluebell of my
choice. At luncheon the English butler lifted him into his
chair and tied on his bib with as much manner as though he
were serving a prince of the blood. The butler has lately
come from the household of the Earl of Durham, Punch from
a cellar in Houston Street. It was a very uplifting spectacle.

My hostesses entertained me afterward with excerpts from
their table conversations of the last two weeks. (I wonder
the butler hasn't given notice; he looked like a respectable
man.) If nothing more comes of it, at least Punch has furnished them with funny stories for the rest of their lives. One
of them is even thinking of writing a book. "At least," says
she, wiping hysterical tears from her eyes, "we have lived!"

The Hon. Cy dropped in at 6:30 last night, and found me
in an evening gown, starting for a dinner at Mrs. Livermore's
house. He mildly observed that Mrs. Lippett did not aspire
to be a society-leader, but saved her energy for her work. You
know I'm not vindictive, but I never look at that man without wishing he were at the bottom of the duck-pond, se-
curely anchored to a rock. Otherwise he'd pop up and float.

Singapore respectfully salutes you, and is very glad that
you can't see him as he now appears. A shocking calamity

has befallen his good looks. Some bad child—and I don't think she's a boy—has clipped that poor beastie in spots, until he looks like a mangy, moth-eaten checkerboard. No one can imagine who did it. Sadie Kate is very handy with the scissors, but she is also handy with an alibi! During the time when the clipping presumably occurred, she was occupying a stool in the corner of the school-room with her face to the wall, as twenty-eight children can testify. However, it has become Sadie Kate's daily duty to treat those spots with your hair tonic.

I am, as usual,
SALLIE.

P.S. This is a recent portrait of the Hon. Cy drawn from life. The man, in some respects, is a fascinating talker; he makes gestures with his nose.

Thursday evening.

Dear Judy:

Sandy is back after a ten-days' absence,—no explanations,
—and plunged deep into gloom. He resents our amiable
efforts to cheer him up, and will have nothing to do with
any of us except baby Allegra. He took her to his house
for supper to-night and never brought her back until
half-past seven, a scandalous hour for a young miss of
three. I don't know what to make of our doctor; he grows
more incomprehensible every day.

But Percy, now, is an open-minded, confiding young
man. He has just been making a dinner-call (he is very
punctilious in all social matters), and our entire conversation was devoted to the girl in Detroit. He is lonely and
likes to talk about her; and the wonderful things he says! I
hope that Miss Detroit is worthy of all this fine affection,
but I'm afraid. He fetched out a leather case from the
innermost recesses of his waistcoat and, reverently un-
wrapping two layers of tissue-paper, showed me the photograph of a silly little thing, all eyes and ear-rings and fuzzy
hair. I did my best to appear congratulatory, but my heart
shut up out of pity for the poor boy's future.

Isn't it funny how the nicest men often choose the
worst wives, and the nicest women the worst husbands?
Their very niceness, I suppose, makes them blind and
unsuspicious.

You know, the most interesting pursuit in the world is
studying character. I believe I was meant to be a novelist;
people fascinate me—until I know them thoroughly. Percy
and the doctor form a most engaging contrast. You always

191

know at any moment what that nice young man is thinking about; he is written like a primer in big type and
one-syllable words. But the doctor! He might as well be
written in Chinese so far as legibility goes. You have
heard of people with a dual nature; well, Sandy possesses a
triple one. Usually he's scientific and as hard as granite,
but occasionally I suspect him of being quite a sentimental
person underneath his official casing. For days at a time he
will be patient and kind and helpful, and I begin to like
him; then without any warning an untamed wild man
swells up from the innermost depths, and—oh, dear! the
creature's impossible.

I always suspect that sometime in the past he has suffered a terrible hurt, and that he is still brooding over the
memory of it. All the time he is talking you have the
uncomfortable feeling that in the far back corners of his
mind he is thinking something else. But this may be
merely my romantic interpretation of an uncommonly bad
temper. In any case, he's baffling.

We have been waiting for a week for a fine windy
afternoon, and this is it. My children are enjoying "kite-
day," a leaf taken from Japan. All of the big-enough boys
and most of the girls are spread over "Knowltop" (that
high, rocky sheep-pasture which joins us on the east)
flying kites made by themselves.

I had a dreadful time coaxing the crusty old gentleman
who owns the estate into granting permission. He doesn't
like orphans, he says, and if he once lets them get a start
in his grounds, the place will be infested with them forever. You would think, to hear him talk, that orphans
were a pernicious kind of beetle.

But after half an hour's persuasive talking on my part,

he grudgingly made us free of his sheep-pasture for two
hours, provided we didn't step foot into the cow-pasture
over the lane, and came home promptly when our time
was up. To insure the sanctity of his cow-pasture, Mr.
Knowltop has sent his gardener and chauffeur and two
grooms to patrol its boundaries while the flying is on. The
children are still at it, and are having a wonderful adventure racing over that windy height and getting tangled up
in one another's strings. When they come panting back
they are to have a surprise in the shape of ginger cookies
and lemonade.

These pitiful little youngsters with their old faces! It's a
difficult task to make them young, but I believe I'm
accomplishing it. And it really is fun to feel you're doing
something positive for the good of the world. If I don't
fight hard against it, you'll be accomplishing your purpose
of turning me into a useful person. The social excitements
of Worcester almost seem tame before the engrossing interest of 113 live, warm, wriggling little orphans.

Yours with love,
SALLIE.

P.S. I believe, to be accurate, that it's 107 children I
possess this afternoon.

Dear Judy:

This being Sunday and a beautiful blossoming day, with a warm wind blowing, I sat at my window with the "Hygiene of the Nervous System" (Sandy's latest contribution to my mental needs) open in my lap, and my eyes on the prospect without. "Thank Heaven!" thought I, "that this institution was so commandingly placed that at least we can look out over the cast-iron wall which shuts us in."

I was feeling very cooped-up and imprisoned and like an orphan myself; so I decided that my own nervous system required fresh air and exercise and adventure. Straight before me ran that white ribbon of road that dips into the valley and up over the hills on the other side. Ever since I came I have longed to follow it to the top and find out what lies beyond those hills. Poor Judy! I dare say that very same longing enveloped your childhood. If any one of my little chicks ever stands by the window and looks across the valley to the hills and asks, "What's over there?" I shall telephone for a motor-car.

But to-day my chicks were all piously engaged with their little souls, I the only wanderer at heart. I changed my silken Sunday gown for homespun, planning meanwhile a means to get to the top of those hills.

Then I went to the telephone and brazenly called up 505.

"Good afternoon, Mrs. McGurk," said I, very sweet. "May I be speaking with Dr. MacRae?"

"Howld the wire," said she, very short.

"Afternoon, Doctor," said I to him. "Have ye, by chance, any dying patients who live on the top o' the hills beyant?"

"I have not, thank the Lord!"

195

" 'T is a pity," said I, disappointed. "And what are ye afther doin' with yerself the day?"

"I am reading the 'Origin of Species.' "

"Shut it up; it's not fit for Sunday. And tell me now, is yer motor-car iled and ready to go?"

"It is at your disposal. Are you wanting me to take some orphans for a ride?"

"Just one who's sufferin' from a nervous system. She's taken a fixed idea that she must get to the top o' the hills."

"My car is a grand climber. In fifteen minutes—"

"Wait!" said I. "Bring with ye a frying-pan that's a decent size for two. There's nothing in my kitchen smaller than a cart-wheel. And ask Mrs. McGurk can ye stay out for supper."

So I packed in a basket a jar of bacon and some eggs and muffins and ginger cookies, with hot coffee in the thermos-bottle, and was waiting on the steps when Sandy chugged up with his automobile and frying-pan.

We really had a beautiful adventure, and he enjoyed the sensation of running away exactly as much as I. Not once did I let him mention insanity. I made him look at the wide stretches of meadow and the lines of pollard willows backed by billowing hills, and sniff the air, and listen to the cawing crows and the tinkle of cow-bells and the gurgling of the river. And we talked—oh, about a million things far removed from our asylum. I made him throw away the idea that he is a scientist, and pretend to be a boy. You will scarcely credit the assertion, but he succeeded—more or less. He did pull off one or two really boyish pranks. Sandy is not yet out of his thirties, and, mercy! that is too early to be grown up.

We camped on a bluff overlooking our view, gathered some driftwood, built a fire, and cooked the *nicest* supper—a sprinkling of burnt stick in our fried eggs, but charcoal's healthy. Then, when Sandy had finished his pipe and "the sun was setting in its wonted west," we packed up and coasted back home.

He says it was the nicest afternoon he has had in years, and, poor deluded man of science, I actually believe it's true. His olive-green home is so uncomfortable and dreary and uninspiring that I don't wonder he drowns his troubles in books. Just as soon as I can find a nice comfortable house-mother to put in charge, I am going to plot for the dismissal of Maggie McGurk, though I foresee that she will be even harder than Sterry to pry from her moorings.

Please don't draw the conclusion that I am becoming unduly interested in our bad-tempered doctor, for I'm not. It's just that he leads such a comfortless life that I sometimes long to pat him on the head and tell him to cheer up; the world's full of sunshine, and some of it's for him—just as I long to comfort my hundred and seven orphans; so much and no more.

I am sure that I had some real news to tell you, but it has completely gone out of my head. The rush of fresh air has made me sleepy. It's half-past nine, and I bid you good night.

S.

P.S. Gordon Hallock has evaporated into thin air. Not a word for three weeks; no candy or stuffed animals or tokimentoes of any description. What on earth do you suppose has become of that attentive young man?

Dearest Judy:

Hark to the glad tidings!

This being the thirty-first day of Punch's month, I telephoned to his two patronesses, as nominated in the bond, to arrange for his return. I was met by an indignant refusal. Give up their sweet little volcano just as they are getting it trained not to belch forth fire? They are out-raged that I can make such an ungrateful request. Punch has accepted their invitation to spend the summer.

The dressmaking is still going on; you should hear the machines whir and the tongues clatter in the sewing-room. Our most cowed, apathetic, spiritless little orphan cheers up and takes an interest in life when she hears that she is to possess three perfectly private dresses of her own, and each a different color, chosen by herself. And you should see how it encourages their sewing ability; even the little ten-year-olds are bursting into seamstresses. I wish I could devise an equally effective way to make them take an interest in cooking. But our kitchen is extremely uneducative: you know how hampering it is to one's en-thusiasm to have to prepare a bushel of potatoes at once.

I think you've heard me mention the fact that I should like to divide up my kiddies into ten nice little families, with a nice comfortable house-mother over each? If we just had ten picturesque cottages to put them in, with flowers in the front yard and rabbits and kittens and puppies and chickens in the back, we should be a perfectly presentable institution, and wouldn't be ashamed to have these charity experts come visiting us.

Thursday.

I started this letter three days ago, was interrupted to talk to a potential philanthropist (fifty tickets to the circus), and have not had time to pick up my pen since. Betsy has been in Philadelphia for three days, being a bridesmaid for a miserable cousin. I hope that no more of her family are thinking of getting married, for it's most upsetting to the J. G. H.

While there, she investigated a family who had applied for a child. Of course we haven't a proper investigating plant, but once in a while, when a family drops right into our arms, we do like to put the business through. As a usual thing, we work with the State Charities' Aid Association. They have a lot of trained agents traveling about the State, keeping in touch with families who are willing to take children, and with asylums that have them to give. Since they are willing to work for us, there is no slightest use in our going to the expense of peddling our own babies. And I do want to place out as many as are available, for I firmly believe that a private home is the best thing for the child, provided, of course, that we are very fussy about the character of the homes we choose. I don't require rich foster-parents, but I do require kind, loving, intelligent parents. This time I think Betsy has landed a gem of a family. The child is not yet delivered or the papers signed, and of course there is always danger that they may give a sudden flop, and splash back into the water.

Ask Jervis if he ever heard of J. F. Bretland of Philadelphia. He seems to move in financial circles. The first I ever heard of him was a letter addressed to the "Supt.

John Grier Home, Dear Sir,"—a curt, typewritten, businesslike letter, from an *awfully* businesslike lawyer, saying that his wife had determined to adopt a baby girl of attractive appearance and good health between the ages of two and three years. The child must be an orphan of American stock, with unimpeachable heredity, and no relatives to interfere. Could I furnish one as required and oblige, yours truly, J. F. Bretland?

By way of reference he mentioned "Bradstreets." Did you ever hear of anything so funny? You would think he was opening a charge-account at a nursery, and enclosing an order from our seed catalogue.

We began our usual investigation by mailing a reference-blank to a clergyman in Germantown, where the J. F. B.'s reside.

Does he own any property?

Does he pay his bills?

Is he kind to animals?

Does he attend church?

Does he quarrel with his wife? And a dozen other impertinent questions.

We evidently picked a clergyman with a sense of humor. Instead of answering in laborious detail, he wrote up and down and across the sheet, "I wish they'd adopt me!"

This looked promising, so B. Kindred obligingly dashed out to Germantown as soon as the wedding breakfast was over. She is developing the most phenomenal detective instinct. In the course of a social call she can absorb from the chairs and tables a family's entire moral history.

She returned from Germantown bursting with enthusiastic details.

Mr. J. F. Bretland is a wealthy and influential citizen,

cordially loved by his friends and deeply hated by his enemies (discharged employees, who do not hesitate to say that he is a *har-rd* man). He is a little shaky in his attendance at church, but his wife seems regular, and he gives money.

She is a charming, kindly, cultivated gentlewoman, just out of a sanatorium after a year of nervous prostration. The doctor says that what she needs is some strong interest in life, and advises adopting a child. She has always longed to do it, but her hard husband has stubbornly refused. But finally, as always, it is the gentle, persistent wife who has triumphed, and hard husband has been forced to give in. Waiving his own natural preference for a boy, he wrote, as above, the usual request for a blue-eyed girl.

Mrs. Bretland, with the firm intention of taking a child, has been reading up for years, and there is no detail of infant dietetics that she does not know. She has a sunny nursery, with a southwestern exposure, all ready. And a closet full of surreptitiously gathered dolls! She has made the clothes for them herself,—she showed them to Betsy with the greatest pride,—so you can understand the necessity for a girl.

She has just heard of an excellent English trained nurse that she can secure, but she isn't sure but that it would be better to start with a French nurse, so that the child can learn the language before her vocal cords are set. Also, she was extremely interested when she heard that Betsy was a college woman. She couldn't make up her mind whether to send the baby to college or not. What was Betsy's honest opinion? If the child were Betsy's own daughter, would Betsy send her to college?

All this would be funny if it weren't so pathetic; but really I can't get away from the picture of that poor lonely woman sewing those doll-clothes for the little unknown girl that she wasn't sure she could have. She lost her own two babies years ago, or, rather, she never had them; they were never alive.

You can see what a good home it's going to be. There's lots of love waiting for the little mite, and that is better than all the wealth which, in this case, goes along.

But the problem now is to find the child, and that isn't easy; the J. F. Bretlands are so abominably explicit in their requirements. I have just the baby boy to give them; but with that closetful of dolls, he is impossible. Little Florence won't do—one tenacious parent living. I've a wide variety of foreigners with liquid brown eyes—won't do at all. Mrs. Bretland is a blonde, and daughter must resemble her. I have several sweet little mites with unspeakable heredity, but the Bretlands want six generations of church-attending grandparents, with a colonial governor at the top. Also I have a darling little curly-headed girl (and curls are getting rarer and rarer), but illegitimate. And that seems to be an unsurmountable barrier in the eyes of adopting parents, though, as a matter of fact, it makes no slightest difference in the child. However, she won't do; the Bretlands hold out sternly for a marriage-certificate.

There remains just one child out of all these one hundred and seven that appears available. Our little Sophie's father and mother were killed in a railroad accident, and the only reason she wasn't killed was because they had just left her in a hospital to get an abscess cut out of her throat. She comes from good common American stock, irreproachable and uninteresting in every way. She's a

washed-out, spiritless, whiney little thing. The doctor has
been pouring her full of his favorite cod-liver oil and
spinach, but he can't get any cheerfulness into her.

However, individual love and care does accomplish wonders in institution children, and she may bloom into
something rare and beautiful after a few months' trans-
planting. So I yesterday wrote a glowing account of her
immaculate family history to J. F. Bretland, offering to
deliver her in Germantown.

This morning I received a telegram from J. F. B. Not at
all! He does not purpose to buy any daughter sight unseen.
He will come and inspect the child in person at three
o'clock on Wednesday next.

Oh dear, if he shouldn't like her! We are now bending
all our energies toward enhancing that child's beauty—
like a pup bound for the dog show. Do you think it would
be awfully immoral if I rouged her cheeks a suspicion? She
is too young to pick up the habit.

Heavens! what a letter! A million pages written without
a break. You can see where my heart is. I'm as excited
over little Sophie's settling in life as though she were my
own darling daughter.

Respectful regards to the president.

SAL. MCB.

Dear Gordon:

That was an obnoxious, beastly, low-down trick not to send me a cheering line for four weeks just because, in a period of abnormal stress, I once let you go for three. I had really begun to be worried for fear you'd tumbled into the Potomac. My chicks would miss you dreadfully; they love their Uncle Gordon. Please remember that you promised to send them a donkey.

Please also remember that I'm a busier person than you. It's a lot harder to run the John Grier Home than the House of Representatives. Besides, you have more efficient people to help.

This isn't a letter; it's an indignant remonstrance. I'll write to-morrow—or the next day.

S.

P.S. On reading your letter over again I am slightly mollified, but dinna think I believe a' your saft words. I ken weel ye only flatter when ye speak sae fair.

Dear Judy:

I have a history to recount.

This, please remember, is Wednesday next. So at half-past two o'clock our little Sophie was bathed and brushed and clothed in fine linen, and put in charge of a trusty orphan, with anxious instructions to keep her clean.

At three-thirty to the minute—never have I known a human being so disconcertingly businesslike as J. F. Bretland—an automobile of expensive foreign design rolled up to the steps of this imposing château. A square-shouldered, square-jawed personage, with a chopped-off mustache and a manner that inclines one to hurry, presented himself three minutes later at my library door. He greeted me briskly as "Miss McKosh." I gently corrected him, and he changed to "Miss McKim." I indicated my most soothing armchair, and invited him to take some light refreshment after his journey. He accepted a glass of water (I admire a temperate parent), and evinced an impatient desire to be done with the business. So I rang the bell and ordered the little Sophie to be brought down.

"Hold on, Miss McGee!" said he to me. "I'd rather see her in her own environment. I will go with you to the playroom or corral or wherever you keep your youngsters."

So I led him to the nursery, where thirteen or fourteen mites in gingham rompers were tumbling about on mattresses on the floor. Sophie, alone in the glory of feminine petticoats, was ensconced in the blue-ginghamed arms of a very bored orphan. She was squirming and fighting to get down, and her feminine petticoats were tightly wound

205

about her neck. I took her in my arms, smoothed her clothes, wiped her nose, and invited her to look at the gentleman.

That child's whole future hung upon five minutes of sunniness, and instead of a single smile, she *whined!*

Mr. Bretland shook her hand in a very gingerly fashion and chirruped to her as you might to a pup. Sophie took not the slightest notice of him, but turned her back, and buried her face in my neck. He shrugged his shoulders, supposed that they could take her on trial. She might suit his wife; he himself didn't want one, anyway. And we turned to go out.

Then who should come toddling straight across his path but that little sunbeam Allegra! Exactly; in front of him she staggered, threw her arms about like a windmill, and plumped down on all fours. He hopped aside with great agility to avoid stepping on her, and then picked her up and set her on her feet. She clasped her arms about his leg, and looked up at him with a gurgling laugh.

"Daddy! Frow baby up!"

He is the first man, barring the doctor, whom the child has seen for weeks, and evidently he resembles somewhat her almost forgotten father.

J. F. Bretland picked her up and tossed her in the air as handily as though it were a daily occurrence, while she ecstatically shrieked her delight. Then when he showed signs of lowering her, she grasped him by an ear and a nose, and drummed a tattoo on his stomach with both feet. No one could ever accuse Allegra of lacking vitality!

J. F. disentangled himself from her endearments, and emerged, rumpled as to hair, but with a firm-set jaw. He set her on her feet, but retained her little doubled-up fist.

"This is the kid for me," he said. "I don't believe I need look any further."

I explained that we couldn't separate little Allegra from her brothers; but the more I objected, the stubborner his jaw became. We went back to the library, and argued about it for half an hour.

He liked her heredity, he liked her looks, he liked her spirit, he liked *her*. If he was going to have a daughter foisted on him, he wanted one with some ginger. He'd be hanged if he'd take that other whimpering little thing. It wasn't natural. But if I gave him Allegra, he would bring her up as his own child, and see that she was provided for for the rest of her life. Did I have any right to cut her out from all that just for a lot of sentimental nonsense? The family was already broken up; the best I could do for them now was to provide for them individually.

"Take all three," said I, quite brazenly.

But, no, he couldn't consider that; his wife was an invalid, and one child was all that she could manage.

Well, I was in a dreadful quandary. It seemed such a chance for the child, and yet it did seem so cruel to separate her from those two adoring little brothers. I knew that if the Bretlands adopted her legally, they would do their best to break all ties with the past, and the child was still so tiny she would forget her brothers as quickly as she had her father.

Then I thought about you, Judy, and of how bitter you have always been because, when that family wanted to adopt you, the asylum wouldn't let you go. You have always said that you might have had a home, too, like other children, but that Mrs. Lippett stole it away from you. Was I perhaps stealing little Allegra's home from her?

With the two boys it would be different; they could be educated and turned out to shift for themselves. But to a girl a home like this would mean everything. Ever since baby Allegra came to us, she has seemed to me just such another child as baby Judy must have been. She has ability and spirit. We must somehow furnish her with opportunity. She, too, deserves her share of the world's beauty and good—as much as nature has fitted her to appreciate. And could any asylum ever give her that? I stood and thought and thought while Mr. Bretland impatiently paced the floor.

"You have those boys down and let me talk to them," Mr. Bretland insisted. "If they have a spark of generosity, they'll be glad to let her go."

I sent for them, but my heart a solid lump of lead. They were still missing their father; it seemed merciless to snatch away that darling baby sister, too.

They came hand in hand, sturdy, fine little chaps, and stood solemnly at attention, with big, wondering eyes fixed on the strange gentleman.

"Come here, boys. I want to talk to you." He took each by a hand. "In the house I live in we haven't any little baby, so my wife and I decided to come here, where there are so many babies without fathers and mothers, and take one home to be ours. She will have a beautiful house to live in, and lots of toys to play with, and she will be happy all her life—much happier than she could ever be here. I know that you will be very glad to hear that I have chosen your little sister."

"And won't we ever see her any more?" asked Clifford.

"Oh, yes, sometimes."

Clifford looked from me to Mr. Bretland, and two

big tears began rolling down his cheeks. He jerked his hand away and came and hurled himself into my arms.

"Don't let him have her! Please! Please! Send him away!"

"Take them all!" I begged.

But he's a hard man.

"I didn't come for an entire asylum," said he, shortly.

By this time Don was sobbing on the other side. And then who should inject himself into the hubbub but Dr. MacRae, with baby Allegra in his arms!

I introduced them, and explained. Mr. Bretland reached for the baby, and Sandy held her tight.

"Quite impossible," said Sandy, shortly. "Miss McBride will tell you that it's one of the rules of this institution never to separate a family."

"Miss McBride has already decided," said J. F. B., stiffly. "We have fully discussed the question."

"You must be mistaken," said Sandy, becoming his Scotchest, and turning to me. "You surely had no intention of performing any such cruelty as this?"

Here was the decision of Solomon all over again, with two of the stubbornest men that the good Lord ever made wresting poor little Allegra limb from limb.

I despatched the three chicks back to the nursery and returned to the fray. We argued loud and hotly, until finally J. F. B. echoed my own frequent query of the last five months: "Who is the head of this asylum, the superintendent or the visiting physician?"

I was furious with the doctor for placing me in such a position before that man, but I couldn't quarrel with him in public; so I had ultimately to tell Mr. Bretland, with finality and flatness, that Allegra was out of the question. Would he not reconsider Sophie?

No, he'd be darned if he'd reconsider Sophie. Allegra or nobody. He hoped that I realized that I had weakly allowed the child's entire future to be ruined. And with that parting shot he backed to the door. "Miss MacRae, Dr. McBride, good afternoon." He achieved two formal bows and withdrew.

And the moment the door closed Sandy and I fought it out. He said that any person who claimed to have any modern, humane views on the subject of childcare ought to be ashamed to have considered for even a moment the question of breaking up such a family; and I accused him of keeping her for the purely selfish reason that he was fond of the child and didn't wish to lose her. (And that, I believe, is the truth.) Oh, we had the battle of our career, and he finally took himself off with a stiffness and politeness that excelled J. F. B.'s.

Between the two of them I feel as limp as though I'd been run through our new mangling-machine. And then Betsy came home, and reviled me for throwing away the choicest family we have ever discovered!

So this is the end of our week of feverish activity; and both Sophie and Allegra are, after all, to be institution children. Oh dear! oh dear! Please remove Sandy from the staff, and send me, instead, a German, a Frenchman a Chinaman, if you choose—anything but a Scotchman.

Yours wearily,
SALLIE.

P.S. I dare say that Sandy is also passing a busy evening in writing to have me removed. I won't object if you wish to do it. I am tired of institutions.

Dear Gordon:

You are a captious, caviling, carping, crabbed, contentious, cantankerous chap. Hoot mon! an' why shouldna I drap into Scotch gin I choose? An' I with a Mac in my name.

Of course the John Grier will be delighted to welcome you on Thursday next, not only for the donkey, but for your sweet sunny presence as well. I was planning to write you a mile-long letter to make up for past deficiencies, but wha's the use? I'll be seeing you the morn's morn, an' unco gude will be the sight o' you for sair een.

Dinna fash yoursel, Laddie, because o' my language. My forebears were from the Hielands.

McBride.

211

Dear Judy:

All's well with the John Grier—except for a broken tooth, a sprained wrist, a badly scratched knee, and one case of pink-eye. Betsy and I are being polite, but cool,

Red hair

S M^c B— cramming up on politics as Gordon is coming

toward the doctor. The annoying thing is that he is rather cool, too; and he seems to be under the impression that the drop in temperature is all on his side. He goes about

his business in a scientific, impersonal way, entirely cour-
teous, but somewhat detached.

However, the doctor is not disturbing us very extensively
at present. We are about to receive a visit from a far more
fascinating person than Sandy. The House of Representatives again rests from its labors, and Gordon enjoys a
vacation, two days of which he is planning to spend at the
Brantwood Inn.

I am delighted to hear that you have had enough sea-
side, and are considering our neighborhood for the rest of
the summer. There are several spacious estates to be had
within a few miles of the John Grier, and it will be a nice
change for Jervis to come home only at week-ends. After
a pleasantly occupied absence, you will each have some
new ideas to add to the common stock.

I can't add any further philosophy just now on the
subject of married life, having to refresh my memory on
the Monroe Doctrine and one or two other political topics.

I am looking eagerly forward to August and three months
with you.

As ever,
SALLIE.

Dear Enemy:

It's very forgiving of me to invite you to dinner after that volcanic explosion of last week. However, please come. You remember our philanthropic friend, Mr. Hallock, who sent us the peanuts and goldfish and other indigestible trifles? He will be with us to-night, so this is your chance to turn the stream of his benevolence into more hygienic channels.

We dine at seven.

As ever,
SALLIE MCBRIDE.

Dear Enemy:

You should have lived in the days when each man inhabited a separate cave on a separate mountain.

S. MCBRIDE.

Dear Judy:

Gordon is here, and a reformed man so far as his attitude toward my asylum goes. He has discovered the world-old truth that the way to a mother's heart is through praise of her children, and he had nothing but praise for all 107 of mine. Even in the case of Loretta Higgins he found something pleasant to say; he thinks it nice that she isn't cross-eyed.

He went shopping with me in the village this afternoon, and was very helpful about picking out hair-ribbons for a couple of dozen little girls. He begged to choose Sadie Kate's himself, and after many hesitations he hit upon orange satin for one braid and emerald-green for the other.

While we were immersed in this business I became aware of a neighboring customer, ostensibly engaged with hooks and eyes, but straining every ear to listen to our nonsense.

She was so dressed up in a picture-hat, a spotted veil, a feather boa, and a *nouveau art* parasol that I never dreamed she was any acquaintance of mine till I happened to catch her eye with a familiar malicious gleam in it. She bowed stiffly, and disapprovingly; and I nodded back. Mrs. Maggie McGurk in her company clothes!

That is a pleasanter expression than she really has. Her smile is due to a slip of the pen.

Poor Mrs. McGurk can't understand any possible intellectual interest in a man. She suspects me of wanting to marry every single one that I meet. At first she thought I

Mrs. McGurk

Red and green parrot

wanted to snatch away her doctor; but now, after seeing me with Gordon, she considers me a bigamous monster who wants them both.

Good-by; some guests approach.

11:30 P.M.

I have just been giving a dinner for Gordon, with Betsy and Mrs. Livermore and Mr. Witherspoon as guests. I graciously included the doctor, but he curtly declined on the ground that he wasn't in a social mood. Our Sandy does not let politeness interfere with truth!

There is no doubt about it, Gordon is the most pre-

sentable man that ever breathed. He is so good-looking
and easy and gracious and witty, and his manners are so
impeccable— Oh, he would make a wonderfully decorative
husband! But after all, I suppose you do live with a
husband; you don't just show him off at dinners and teas.

He was exceptionally nice to-night. Betsy and Mrs.
Livermore both fell in love with him—and I just a trifle.
He entertained us with a speech in his best public manner, apropos of Java's welfare. We have been having a
dreadful time finding a sleeping-place for that monkey,
and Gordon proved with incontestable logic that, since he
was presented to us by Jimmie, and Jimmie is Percy's
friend, he should sleep with Percy. Gordon is a natural
talker, and an audience affects him like champagne. He
can argue with as much emotional earnestness on the
subject of a monkey as on the greatest hero that ever bled
for his country.

I felt tears coming to my eyes when he described Java's
loneliness as he watched out the night in our furnace
cellar, and pictured his brothers at play in the far-off
tropical jungle.

A man who can talk like that has a future before him. I
haven't a doubt but that I shall be voting for him for
President in another twenty years.

We all had a beautiful time, and entirely forgot—for a
space of three hours—that 107 orphans slumbered about
us. Much as I love the little dears, it is pleasant to get
away from them once in a while.

My guests left at ten, and it must be midnight by now.
(This is the eighth day, and my clock has stopped again;
Jane forgets to wind it as regularly as Friday comes around.)
However, I know it's late; and as a woman, it's my duty to

try for beauty sleep, especially with an eligible young suitor at hand.

I'll finish to-morrow. Good night.

Saturday.

Gordon spent this morning playing with my asylum and planning some intelligent presents to be sent later. He thinks that three neatly painted totem-poles would add to the attractiveness of our Indian camps. He is also going to make us a present of three dozen pink rompers for the babies. Pink is a color that is very popular with the superintendent of this asylum, who is deadly tired of blue! Our generous friend is likewise amusing himself with the idea of a couple of donkeys and saddles and a little red cart. Isn't it nice that Gordon's father provided for him so amply, and that he is such a charitably inclined young man? He is at present lunching with Percy at the hotel, and, I trust, imbibing fresh ideas in the field of philanthropy.

Perhaps you think I haven't enjoyed this interruption to the monotony of institution life! You can say all you please, my dear Mrs. Pendleton, about how well I am managing your asylum, but, just the same, it isn't natural for me to be so stationary. I very frequently need a change. That is why Gordon, with his bubbling optimism and boyish spirits, is so exhilarating, especially as a contrast to too much doctor.

Sunday morning.

I must tell you the end of Gordon's visit. His intention had been to leave at four, but in an evil moment I begged him to stay over till 9:30, and yesterday afternoon he and

Singapore and I took a long 'cross-country walk, far out of
sight of the towers of this asylum, and stopped at a pretty
little roadside inn, where we had a satisfying supper of
ham and eggs and cabbage. Sing stuffed so disgracefully
that he has been languid ever since.

The walk and all was fun, and a very grateful change
from this monotonous life I lead. It would have kept me
pleasant and contented for weeks if something most unpleasant hadn't happened later. We had a beautiful, sunny,
care-free afternoon, and I'm sorry to have had it spoiled.
We came back very unromantically in the trolley-car, and
reached the J. G. H. before nine, just in good time for
him to run on to the station and catch his train. So I didn't
ask him to come in, but politely wished him a pleasant
journey at the porte-cochère.

A car was standing at the side of the drive, in the
shadow of the house; I recognized it, and thought the
doctor was inside with Mr. Witherspoon. (They frequently
spend their evenings together in the laboratory.) Well,
Gordon, at the moment of parting, was seized with an
unfortunate impulse to ask me to abandon the management of this asylum, and take over the management of a
private house instead.

Did you ever know anything like the man? He had had
the whole afternoon and miles of empty meadow in which
to discuss the question, but instead he must choose our
door-mat!

I don't know just what I did say: I tried to turn it off
lightly and hurry him to his train. But he refused to be
turned off lightly. He braced himself against a post and
insisted upon arguing it out. I knew that he was missing
his train, and that every window in this institution was

open. A man never has the slightest thought of possible overhearers; it is always the woman who thinks of convention.

Being in a nervous twitter to get rid of him, I suppose I was pretty abrupt and tactless. He began to get angry, and then by some unlucky chance his eye fell on that car. He recognized it, too, and, being in a savage mood, he began making fun of the doctor. "Old Goggle-eyes" he called him, and "Scatchy," and oh, the awfullest lot of unmannerly, silly things!

I was assuring him with convincing earnestness that I didn't care a rap about the doctor, that I thought he was just as funny and impossible as he could be, when suddenly the doctor rose out of his car and walked up to us.

I could have evaporated from the earth very comfortably at that moment!

Sandy was quite clearly angry, as well he might be, after the things he'd heard, but he was entirely cold and collected. Gordon was hot, and bursting with imaginary wrongs. I was aghast at this perfectly foolish and unnecessary muddle that had suddenly arisen out of nothing. Sandy apologized to me with unimpeachable politeness for inadvertently overhearing, and then turned to Gordon and stiffly invited him to get into his car and ride to the station.

I begged him not to go. I didn't wish to be the cause of any silly quarrel between them. But without paying the slightest attention to me, they climbed into the car, and whirled away, leaving me placidly standing on the door-mat.

I came in and went to bed, and lay awake for hours, expecting to hear—I don't know what kind of explosion. It is now eleven o'clock, and the doctor hasn't appeared.

I don't know how on earth I shall meet him when he does. I fancy I shall hide in the clothes-closet.

Did you ever know anything as unnecessary and stupid as this whole situation? I suppose now I've quarreled with Gordon,—and I positively don't know over what,—and of course my relations with the doctor are going to be terribly awkward. I said horrid things about him,—you know the silly way I talk,—things I didn't mean in the least.

I wish it were yesterday at this time. I would make Gordon go at four.

SALLIE.

Sunday afternoon.

Dear Dr. MacRae:

That was a horrid, stupid, silly business last night. But by this time you must know me well enough to realize that I never mean the foolish things I say. My tongue has no slightest connection with my brain; it just runs along by itself. I must seem to you very ungrateful for all the help you have given me in this unaccustomed work and for the patience you have (occasionally) shown.

I do appreciate the fact that I could never have run this asylum by myself without your responsible presence in the background; and though once in a while, as you yourself must acknowledge, you have been pretty impatient and bad tempered and difficult, still I have never held it up against you, and I really didn't mean any of the ill-mannered things I said last night. Please forgive me for being rude. I should hate very much to lose your friendship. And we are friends, are we not? I like to think so.

S. McB.

Dear Judy:

I am sure I haven't an idea whether or not the doctor and I have made up our differences. I sent him a polite note of apology, which he received in abysmal silence. He didn't come near us until this afternoon, and he hasn't by the blink of an eyelash referred to our unfortunate contretemps. We talked exclusively about an ichthyol salve that will remove eczema from a baby's scalp; then, Sadie Kate being present, the conversation turned to cats. It seems that the doctor's Maltese cat has four kittens, and Sadie Kate will not be silenced until she has seen them. Before I knew what was happening I found myself making an engagement to take her to see those miserable kittens at four o'clock to-morrow afternoon.

Whereupon the doctor, with an indifferently polite bow, took himself off. And that apparently is the end.

Your Sunday note arrives, and I am delighted to hear that you have taken the house. It will be beautiful having you for a neighbor for so long. Our improvements ought to march along, with you and the president at our elbow. But it does seem as though you ought to get out here before August 7. Are you sure that city air is good for you just now? I have never known so devoted a wife.

My respects to the president.

                                                                S. McB

Dear Judy:

Please listen to this!

At four o'clock I took Sadie Kate to the doctor's house to look at those cats. But Freddy Howland just twenty minutes before had fallen down-stairs, so the doctor was at the Howland house occupying himself with Freddy's collar-bone. He had left word for us to sit down and wait, that he would be back shortly.

Mrs. McGurk ushered us into the library; and then, not to leave us alone, came in herself on a pretense of polishing the brass. I don't know what she thought we'd do! Run off with the pelican perhaps.

I settled down to an article about the Chinese situation in the *Century*, and Sadie Kate roamed about at large examining everything she found, like a curious little mongoose.

She commenced with his stuffed flamingo and wanted to know what made it so tall and what made it so red. Did it always eat frogs, and had it hurt its other foot? She ticks off questions with the steady persistency of an eight-day clock.

I buried myself in my article and left Mrs. McGurk to deal with Sadie. Finally, after she had worked half-way around the room, she came to a portrait of a little girl occupying a leather frame in the center of the doctor's writing desk—a child with a queer elf-like beauty, resembling very strangely our little Allegra. This photograph might have been a portrait of Allegra grown five years older. I had noticed the picture the night we took supper

224

with the doctor, and had meant to ask which of his little patients she was. Happily I didn't!

"Who's that?" said Sadie Kate, pouncing upon it.

"It's the docthor's little gurrl."

"Where is she?"

"Shure, she's far away wit' her gran'ma."

"Where'd he get her?"

"His wife give her to him."

I emerged from my book with electric suddenness.

"His wife!" I cried.

The next instant I was furious with myself for having spoken, but I was so completely taken off my guard. Mrs. McGurk straightened up and became volubly conversational at once.

"And didn't he never tell you about his wife? She went insane six years ago. It got so it weren't safe to keep her in the house, and he had to put her away. It near killed him. I never seen a lady more beautiful than her. I guess he didn't so much as smile for a year. It's funny he never told you nothing, and you such a friend!"

"Naturally it's not a subject he cares to talk about," said I dryly, and I asked her what kind of brass polish she used.

Sadie Kate and I went out to the garage and hunted up the kittens ourselves; and we mercifully got away before the doctor came back.

But will you tell me what this means? Didn't Jervis know he was married? It's the queerest thing I ever heard. I do think, as the McGurk suggests, that Sandy might casually have dropped the information that he had a wife in an insane asylum.

But of course it must be a terrible tragedy and I suppose he can't bring himself to talk about it. I see now why he's so morbid over the question of heredity—I dare say he fears for the little girl. When I think of all the jokes I've made on the subject, I'm aghast at how I must have hurt him, and angry with myself and angry with him.

I feel as though I never wanted to see the man again. Mercy! did you ever know such a muddle as we are getting ourselves into?

Yours,
SALLIE.

P.S. Tom McCoomb has pushed Mamie Prout into the box of mortar that the masons use. She's parboiled. I've sent for the doctor.

My *dear Madam*:

I have a shocking scandal to report about the superintendent of the John Grier Home. Don't let it get into the newspapers, please. I can picture the spicy details of the investigation prior to her removal by the "Cruelty."

I was sitting in the sunshine by my open window this morning reading a sweet book on the Froebel theory of child culture—never lose your temper, always speak kindly to the little ones. Though they may appear bad, they are not so in reality. It is either that they are not feeling well or have nothing interesting to do. Never punish; simply deflect their attention. I was entertaining a very loving, uplifted attitude toward all this young life about me when my attention was attracted by a group of little boys beneath the window.

"Aw—John—don't hurt it!"

"Let it go!"

"Kill it quick!"

And above their remonstrances rose the agonized squealing of some animal in pain. I dropped Froebel and, running downstairs, burst upon them from the side door. They saw me coming, and scattered right and left, revealing Johnnie Cobden engaged in torturing a mouse. I will spare you the grisly details. I called to one of the boys to come and drown the creature quick! John I seized by the collar; and dragged him squirming and kicking in at the kitchen door. He is a big, hulking boy of thirteen, and he fought like a little tiger, holding on to posts and doorjambs as we passed. Ordinarily I doubt if I could

227

have handled him, but that one sixteenth Irish that I
possess was all on top, and I was fighting mad. We
burst into the kitchen, and I hastily looked about for
a means of chastisement. The pancake-turner was the
first utensil that met my eyes. I seized it and beat that
child with all my strength, until I had reduced him to
a cowering, whimpering mendicant for mercy, instead
of the fighting little bully he had been four minutes
before.

And then who should suddenly burst into the midst of
this explosion but Dr. MacRae! His face was blank with
astonishment. He strode over and took the pancake-turner
out of my hand and set the boy on his feet. Johnnie got
behind him and clung! I was so angry that I really couldn't
talk; it was all I could do not to cry.

"Come, we will take him up to the office," was all the
doctor said. And we marched out, Johnnie keeping as far
from me as possible and limping conspicuously. We left
him in the outer office, and went into my library and shut
the door.

"What in the world has the child done?" he asked.

At that I simply laid my head down on the table and
began to cry! I was utterly exhausted both emotionally and
physically; it had taken all the strength I possessed to
make the pancake-turner effective.

I sobbed out all the bloody details, and he told me not
to think about it; the mouse was dead now. Then he got
me some water to drink, and told me to keep on crying till
I was tired; it would do me good. I am not sure that he didn't
pat me on the head! Anyway, it was his best professional manner. I have watched him administer the same
treatment a dozen times to hysterical orphans. And this

was the first time in a week that we had spoken beyond
the formality of "good morning"!

Well, as soon as I had got to the stage where I could sit
up and laugh, intermittently dabbing my eyes with a wad
of handkerchief, we began a review of Johnnie's case. The
boy has a morbid heredity, and may be slightly defective,
says Sandy. We must deal with the fact as we would with
any other disease. Even normal boys are often cruel; a
child's moral sense is undeveloped at thirteen.

Then he suggested that I bathe my eyes with hot water
and resume my dignity. Which I did. And we had Johnnie
in. He stood—by preference—through the entire interview. The doctor talked to him, oh, so sensibly and kindly
and humanely! John put up the plea that the mouse was a
pest and ought to be killed. The doctor replied that the
welfare of the human race demanded the sacrifice of many
animals for its own good, not for revenge, but that the
sacrifice must be carried out with the least possible hurt to
the animal. He explained about the mouse's nervous system, and how the poor little creature had no means of
defense. It was a cowardly thing to hurt it wantonly. He
told John to try to develop imagination enough to look at
things from the other person's point of view, even if the
other person was only a mouse. Then he went to the bookcase and took down my copy of Burns, and told the
boy what a great poet he was, and how all Scotchmen
loved his memory.

"And this is what he wrote about a mouse," said Sandy,
turning to the "Wee, sleekit, cow'rin, tim'rous beastie,"
which he read and explained to the lad as only a Scotchman could.

Johnnie departed penitent, and Sandy redirected his

professional attention to me. He said I was tired and in need of a change. Why not go to the Adirondacks for a week? He and Betsy and Mr. Witherspoon would make themselves into a committee to run the asylum.

You know, that's exactly what I was longing to do! I need a shifting of ideas and some pine-scented air. My family opened the camp last week, and think I'm awful not to join them. They *won't* understand that when you accept a position like this you can't casually toss it aside whenever you feel like it. But for a few days I can easily manage. My asylum is wound up like an eight-day clock, and will run until a week from next Monday at 4 P.M., when my train will return me. Then I shall be comfortably settled again before you arrive, and with no errant fancies in my brain.

Meanwhile Master John is in a happily chastened frame of mind and body. And I rather suspect that Sandy's moralizing had the more force because it was preceded by my pancake-turner! But one thing I know—Suzanne Estelle is terrified whenever I step into her kitchen. I casually picked up the potato-masher this morning while I was commenting upon last night's over-salty soup, and she ran to cover behind the woodshed door.

To-morrow at nine I set out on my travels, after preparing the way with five telegrams. And, oh! you can't imagine how I'm looking forward to being a gay, care-free young thing again—to canoeing on the lake and tramping in the woods and dancing at the clubhouse. I was in a state of delirium all night long at the prospect. Really, I hadn't realized how mortally tired I had become of all this asylum scenery.

"What you need," said Sandy to me, "is to get away for a little and sow some wild oats."

That diagnosis was positively clairvoyant. I can't think of anything in the world I'd rather do than sow a few wild oats. I'll come back with fresh energy, ready to welcome you and a busy summer.

As ever,
SALLIE.

P.S. Jimmie and Gordon are both going to be up there. How I wish you could join us! A husband is very discommoding.

Dear Judy:

This is to tell you that the mountains are higher than usual, the woods greener, and the lake bluer.

People seem late about coming up this year; the Harrimans' camp is the only other one at our end of the lake that is open. The club-house is very scantily supplied with dancing-men, but we have as house guest an obliging young politician who likes to dance, so I am not discommoded by the general scarcity.

The affairs of the nation and the rearing of orphans are alike delegated to the background while we paddle about among the lily-pads of this delectable lake. I look forward with reluctance to 7:56 next Monday morning, when I turn my back on the mountains. The awful thing about a vacation is that the moment it begins your happiness is already clouded by its approaching end.

I hear a voice on the veranda asking if Sallie is to be found within or without.

Addio!

S.

Dear Judy:

Back at the John Grier, reshouldering the burdens of the coming generation. What should meet my eyes upon entering these grounds but John Cobden, of pancake-turner memory, wearing a badge upon his sleeve. I turned it to me and read "S. P. C. A." in letters of gold! The doctor, during my absence, has formed a local branch of the Cruelty to Animals, and made Johnnie its president.

I hear that yesterday he stopped the workmen on the foundation for the new farm cottage and scolded them severely for whipping their horses up the incline! None of all this strikes any one but me as funny.

There's a lot of news, but with you due in four days, why bother to write? Just one delicious bit I am saving for the end. So hold your breath. You are going to receive a thrill on page 4. You should hear Sadie Kate squeal! Jane is cutting her hair. Instead of wearing it in two tight braids

like this, our little colleen will in the future look like this:

"Them pigtails got on my nerves," says Jane.

You can see how much more stylish and becoming the present coiffure is. I think somebody will be wanting to adopt her. Only Sadie Kate is such an independent, manly little creature; she is eminently fitted by nature to shift for herself. I must save adopting parents for the helpless ones.

You should see our new clothes! I can't wait for this assemblage of rosebuds to burst upon you. And you should have seen those blue ginghamed eyes brighten when the new frocks were actually given out—three for each girl, all different colors, and all perfectly private personal property, with the owner's indelible name inside the collar. Mrs. Lippett's lazy system of having each child draw from the wash a promiscuous dress each week, was an insult to feminine nature.

Sadie Kate is squealing like a baby pig. I must go to see if Jane has by mistake clipped off an ear.

Jane hasn't. Sadie's excellent ears are still intact. She is just squealing on principle; the way one does in a dentist's chair, under the belief that it is going to hurt the next instant.

I really can't think of anything else to write except my news,—so here it is,—and I hope you'll like it.

I am engaged to be married.

My love to you both.
S. McB.

Dear Judy:

Betsy and I are just back from a *giro* in our new motor-car. It undoubtedly does add to the pleasure of institution life. The car of its own accord turned up Long Ridge Road, and stopped before the gates of Shadywell. The chains were up, and the shutters battened down, and the place looked closed and gloomy and rain-soaked. It wore a sort of fall of the House of Usher air, and didn't in the least resemble the cheerful house that used to greet me hospitably of an afternoon.

I hate to have our nice summer ended. It seems as though a section of my life was shut away behind me, and the unknown future was pressing awfully close. Positively, I'd like to postpone that wedding another six months, but I'm afraid poor Gordon would make too dreadful a fuss. Don't think I'm getting wobbly, for I'm not. It's just that somehow I need more time to think about it, and March is getting nearer every day. I know absolutely that I'm doing the most sensible thing. Everybody, man or woman, is the better for being nicely and appropriately and cheerfully married; but oh dear! oh dear! I do hate upheavals, and this is going to be such a world-without-end upheaval! Sometimes when the day's work is over, and I'm tired, I haven't the spirit to rise and meet it.

And now especially since you've bought Shadywell, and are going to be here every summer, I resent having to leave. Next year, when I'm far away, I'll be consumed with homesickness, thinking of all the busy, happy times at the John Grier, with you and Betsy and Percy and our grumbly Scotchman working away cheerfully without me. How can anything ever make up to a mother for the loss of 107 children?

I trust that Judy, Junior, stood the journey into town without upsetting her usual poise. I am sending her a bit giftie, made partly by myself and chiefly by Jane. But two rows, I must inform you, were done by the doctor. One only gradually plumbs the depths of Sandy's nature. After a ten-months' acquaintance with the man, I discover that he knows how to knit, an accomplishment he picked up in his boyhood from an old shepherd on the Scotch moors.

He dropped in three days ago and stayed for tea, really in almost his old friendly mood. But he has since stiffened up again to the same man of granite we knew all summer. I've given up trying to make him out. I suppose, however, that any one might be expected to be a bit down with a wife in an insane asylum. I wish he'd talk about it once. It's awful having such a shadow hovering in the background of your thoughts and never coming out into plain sight.

I know that this letter doesn't contain a word of the kind of news that you like to hear. But it's that beastly twilight hour of a damp November day, and I'm in a beastly uncheerful mood. I'm awfully afraid that I am developing into a temperamental person, and Heaven knows Gordon can supply all the temperament that one family needs! I don't know where we'll land if I don't preserve my sensibly stolid, cheerful nature.

Have you really decided to go South with Jervis? I appreciate your feeling (to a slight extent) about not

wanting to be separated from a husband; but it does seem
sort of hazardous to me to move so young a daughter to
the tropics.

The children are playing blindman's-buff in the lower
corridor. I think I'll have a romp with them, and try to be
in a more affable mood before resuming my pen.

A bientôt!
SALLIE.

P.S. These November nights are pretty cold, and we are
getting ready to move the camps indoors. Our Indians are
very pampered young savages at present, with a double
supply of blankets and hot-water bottles. I shall hate to
see the camps go; they have done a lot for us. Our lads
will be as tough as Canadian trappers when they come in.

November 20.

Dear Judy:

Your motherly solicitude is sweet, but I didn't mean what I said. Of course it's perfectly safe to convey Judy, Junior, to the temperately tropical lands that are washed by the Caribbean. She'll thrive as long as you don't set her absolutely on top of the equator. And your bungalow, shaded by palms and fanned by sea-breezes, with an ice-machine in the back yard and an English doctor across the bay, sounds made for the rearing of babies.

My objections were all due to the selfish fact that I and the John Grier are going to be lonely without you this winter. I really think it's entrancing to have a husband who engages in such picturesque pursuits as financing tropical railroads and developing asphalt lakes and rubber groves and mahogany forests. I wish that Gordon would take to life in those picturesque countries; I'd be more thrilled by the romantic possibilities of the future. Washington seems awfully commonplace compared with Honduras and Nicaragua and the islands of the Caribbean.

I'll be down to wave good-by.

Addio!
SALLIE.

November 24.

Dear Gordon:

Judy has gone back to town, and is sailing next week for Jamaica, where she is to make her headquarters while Jervis cruises about adjacent waters on these entertaining new ventures of his. Couldn't you engage in traffic in the South Seas? I think I'd feel pleasanter about leaving my asylum if you had something romantic and adventurous to offer instead. And think how beautiful you'd be in those white linen clothes! I really believe I might be able to stay in love with a man quite permanently if he always dressed in white.

You can't imagine how I miss Judy. Her absence leaves a dreadful hole in my afternoons. Can't you run up for a week-end soon? I think the sight of you would be very cheering, and I'm feeling awfully down of late. You know, my dear Gordon, I like you much better when you're right here before my eyes than when I merely think about you from a distance. I believe you must have a sort of hypnotic influence. Occasionally, after you've been away a long time, your spell wears a little thin; but when I see you, it all comes back. You've been away now a long, long time; so, please come fast and bewitch me over again!

S.

December 2.

Dear Judy:

Do you remember in college, when you and I used to plan our favorite futures, how we were forever turning our faces southward? And now to think it has really come true, and you are there, coasting around those tropical isles! Did you ever have such a thrill in the whole of your life, barring one or two connected with Jervis, as when you came up on deck in the early dawn and found yourself riding at anchor in the harbor of Kingston, with the water so blue and the palms so green and the beach so white?

I remember when I first woke in that harbor; I felt like a heroine of grand opera surrounded by untruly beautiful painted scenery. Nothing in my four trips to Europe ever thrilled me like the queer sights and tastes and smells of those three warm weeks seven years ago. And ever since, I've panted to get back. When I stop to think about it, I can hardly bring myself to swallow our unexciting meals; I wish to be dining on curries and tamales and mangos. Isn't it funny? You'd think I must have a dash of Creole or Spanish or some warm blood in me somewhere, but I'm nothing on earth but a chilly mixture of English and Irish and Scotch. Perhaps that is why I hear the South calling. "The palm dreams of the pine, and the pine of the palm."

After seeing you off, I turned back to New York with an awful wander-thirst gnawing at my vitals. I, too, wanted to be starting off on my travels in a new blue hat and a new blue suit with a big bunch of violets in my

241

hand. For five minutes I would cheerfully have said
good-by forever to poor dear Gordon in return for the
wide world to wander in. I suppose you are thinking they
are not entirely incompatible—Gordon and the wide
world—but I don't seem able to get your point of view
about husbands. I see marriage as a man must, a good,
sensible workaday institution; but awfully curbing to
one's liberty. Somehow, after you're married forever,
life has lost its feeling of adventure. There aren't any
romantic possibilities waiting to surprise you around each
corner.

The disgraceful truth is that one man doesn't seem
quite enough for me. I like the variety of sensation
that you get only from a variety of men. I'm afraid I've
spent too flirtatious a youth, and it isn't easy for me
to settle.

I seem to have a very wandering pen. To return: I saw
you off, and took the ferry back to New York with a
horribly empty feeling. After our intimate, gossipy three
months together, it seems a terrible task to tell you my
troubles in tones that will reach to the bottom of the
continent. My ferry slid right under the nose of your
steamer, and I could see you and Jervis plainly leaning on
the rail. I waved frantically, but you never blinked an
eyelash. Your gaze was fixed in homesick contemplation
upon the top of the Woolworth Building.

Back in New York, I took myself to a department store
to accomplish a few trifles in the way of shopping. As I
was entering through their revolving-doors, who should be
revolving in the other direction but Helen Brooks! We had
a terrible time meeting, as I tried to go back out, and she
tried to come back in; I thought we should revolve eter-

nally. But we finally got together and shook hands, and she obligingly helped me choose fifteen dozen pairs of stockings and fifty caps and sweaters and two hundred union suits, and then we gossiped all the way up to Fifty-second Street, where we had luncheon at the Women's University Club.

I always liked Helen. She's not spectacular, but steady and dependable. Will you ever forget the way she took hold of that senior pageant committee and whipped it into shape after Mildred had made such a mess of it? How would she do here as a successor to me? I am filled with jealousy at the thought of a successor, but I suppose I must face it.

"When did you last see Judy Abbott?" was Helen's first question.

"Fifteen minutes ago," said I. "She has just set sail for the Spanish main with a husband and daughter and nurse and maid and valet and dog."

"Has she a nice husband?"

"None better."

"And does she still like him?"

"Never saw a happier marriage."

It struck me that Helen looked a trifle bleak, and I suddenly remembered all that gossip that Marty Keene told us last summer; so I hastily changed the conversation to a perfectly safe subject like orphans.

But later she told me the whole story herself in as detached and impersonal a way as though she were discussing the characters in a book. She has been living alone in the city, hardly seeing any one, and she seemed low in spirits and glad to talk. Poor Helen appears to have made an awful mess of her life. I don't know any one who has covered so much ground in such a short space of time. Since her graduation she has been married, has had a baby and lost him, divorced her husband, quarreled with her family, and come to the city to earn her own living. She is reading manuscript for a publishing house.

There seems to have been no reason for her divorce from the ordinary point of view; the marriage just simply didn't work. They weren't friends. If he had been a woman, she wouldn't have wasted half an hour talking with him. If she had been a man, he would have said: "Glad to see you. How are you?" and gone on. And yet they *married*. Isn't it dreadful how blind this sex business can make people?

She was brought up on the theory that a woman's only legitimate profession is home-making. When she finished college, she was naturally eager to start on her career, and Henry presented himself. Her family scanned him closely, and found him perfect in every respect—good family, good morals, good financial position, good-looking. Helen was in love with him. She had a big wedding and lots of new clothes and dozens of embroidered towels. Everything looked propitious.

But as they began to get acquainted, they didn't like the same books or jokes or people or amusements. He was expansive and social and hilarious, and she wasn't. First they bored, and then they irritated, each other. Her orderliness made him impatient, and his disorderliness drove her wild. She would spend a day getting closets and bureau drawers in order, and in five minutes he would stir them into chaos. He would leave his clothes about for her to pick up, and his towels in a messy heap on the bathroom floor, and he never scrubbed out the tub. And she, on her side, was awfully unresponsive and irritating,—she realized it fully,—she got to the point where she wouldn't laugh at his jokes.

I suppose most old-fashioned, orthodox people would think it awful to break up a marriage on such innocent grounds. It seemed so to me at first; but as she went on piling up detail on detail, each trivial in itself, but making a mountainous total, I agreed with Helen that it was awful to keep it going. It wasn't really a marriage; it was a mistake.

So one morning at breakfast, when the subject of what they should do for the summer came up, she said quite casually that she thought she would go West and get a residence in some State where you could get a divorce for a respectable cause; and for the first time in months he agreed with her.

You can imagine the outraged feelings of her Victorian family. In all the seven generations of their sojourn in America they have never had anything like this to record in the family Bible. It all comes from sending her to college and letting her read such dreadful modern people as Ellen Key and Bernard Shaw.

"If he had only got drunk and dragged me about by the hair," Helen wailed, "it would have been legitimate; but because we didn't actually throw things at each other, no one could see any reason for a divorce."

The pathetic part of the whole business is that both she and Henry were admirably fitted to make some one else happy. They just simply didn't match each other; and when two people don't match, all the ceremonies in the world can't marry them.

Saturday morning.

I meant to get this letter off two days ago; and here I am
with volumes written, but nothing mailed.

We've just had one of those miserable deceiving nights—
cold and frosty when you go to bed, and warm and lifeless
when you wake in the dark, smothered under a mountain
of blankets. By the time I had removed my own extra
covers and plumped up my pillow and settled comfortably,
I thought of those fourteen bundled-up babies in the
fresh-air nursery. Their so-called night nurse sleeps like a
top the whole night through. (Her name is next on the
list to be expunged.) So I roused myself again, and made a
little blanket-removing tour, and by the time I had finished I was forever awake. It is not often that I pass a *nuit
blanche*; but when I do, I settle world problems. Isn't it
funny how much keener your mind is when you are lying
awake in the dark?

I began thinking about Helen Brooks, and I planned
her whole life over again. I don't know why her miserable
story has taken such a hold over me; it's a disheartening
subject for an engaged girl to contemplate. I keep saying
to myself, What if Gordon and I, when we really get
acquainted, should change our minds about liking each
other? The fear grips my heart and wrings it dry. But I am
marrying him for no reason in the world except affection.
I'm not particularly ambitious. Neither his position nor his
money ever tempted me in the least; and certainly I am
not doing it to find my life-work, for in order to marry I
am having to give up the work that I love. I really do love
this work; I go about planning and planning their baby
futures, feeling that I'm constructing the nation. Whatever

becomes of me in after life, I am sure I'll be the more capable for having had this tremendous experience. And it *is* a tremendous experience, the nearness to humanity that an asylum brings. I am learning so many new things every day that when each Saturday night comes I look back on the Sallie of last Saturday night, amazed at her ignorance.

You know I am developing a funny old characteristic; I am getting to hate change. I don't like the prospect of having my life disrupted. I used to love the excitement of volcanoes, but now a high level plateau is my choice in landscape. I am very comfortable where I am; my desk and closet and bureau drawers are organized to suit me; and, oh, I dread unspeakably the thought of the upheaval that is going to happen to me next year! Please don't imagine that I don't care for Gordon quite as much as any man has a right to be cared for. It isn't that I like him any the less, but I am getting to like orphans the more.

I just met our medical adviser a few minutes ago as he was emerging from the nursery—Allegra is the only person in the institution who is favored by his austere social attentions. He paused in passing to make a polite comment upon the sudden change in the weather, and to express the hope that I would remember him to Mrs. Pendleton when I wrote.

This is a miserable letter to send off on its travels, with scarcely a word of the kind of news that you like to hear. But our bare little orphan-asylum up in the hills must seem awfully far away from the palms and orange-groves and lizards and tarantulas that you are enjoying.

Have a good time, and don't forget the John Grier Home
and
SALLIE.

December 11.

Dear Judy:

Your Jamaica letter is here, and I'm glad to learn that Judy, Junior, enjoys traveling. Write me every detail about your house, and send some photographs, so I can see you in it. What fun it must be to have a boat of your own that chugs about those entertaining seas! Have you worn all of your eighteen white dresses yet? And aren't you glad now that I made you wait about buying a Panama hat till you reached Kingston?

We are running along here very much as usual without anything exciting to chronicle. You remember little Maybelle Fuller, don't you—the chorus girl's daughter whom our doctor doesn't like? We have placed her out. I tried to make the woman take Hattie Heaphy instead,— the quiet little one who stole the communion-cup,—but no, indeed! Maybelle's eyelashes won the day. After all, as poor Marie says, the chief thing is to be pretty. All else in life depends on that.

When I got home last week, after my dash to New York, I made a brief speech to the children. I told them that I had just been seeing Aunt Judy off on a big ship, and I am embarrassed to have to report that the interest—at least on the part of the boys—immediately abandoned Aunt Judy and centered upon the ship. How many tons of coal did she burn a day? Was she long enough to reach from the carriage-house to the Indian camp? Were there any guns aboard, and if a privateer should attack her, could she hold her own? In case of a mutiny, could the captain shoot down anybody he chose, and wouldn't he be hanged when he got to shore? I had ignominiously to call upon Sandy to finish my speech. I realize that the best-equipped feminine mind in the world can't cope with the peculiar class of questions that originate in a thirteen-year boy's brain.

As a result of their seafaring interest, the doctor conceived the idea of inviting seven of the oldest and most alert lads to spend the day with him in New York and see with their own eyes an ocean-liner. They rose at five yesterday morning, caught the 7:30 train, and had the most wonderful adventure that has happened in all their seven lives. They visited one of the big liners (Sandy knows the Scotch engineer), and were conducted from the bottom of the hold to the top of the crow's-nest, and then had luncheon on board. And after luncheon they visited the aquarium and the top of the Singer Building, and took the subway up-town to spend an hour with the birds of America in their habitats. Sandy with great difficulty pried them away from the Natural History Museum in time to catch the 6:15 train. Dinner in the dining-car. They inquired with great particularity how much it was costing, and when they heard that it was the same, no matter how much you ate, they drew deep breaths and settled quietly and steadily to the task of not allowing their host to be cheated. The railroad made nothing on that party, and all the tables around stopped eating to stare. One traveler asked the doctor if it was a boarding-school he had in charge; so you can see how the manners and bearing of our lads have picked up. I don't wish to boast, but no one would ever have asked such a question concerning seven of Mrs. Lippett's youngsters. "Are they bound for a reformatory?"

would have been the natural question after observing the table manners of her offspring.

My little band tumbled in toward ten o'clock, excitedly babbling a mess of statistics about reciprocating compound engines and water-tight bulkheads, devil-fish and sky-scrapers and birds of paradise. I thought I should never get them to bed. And, oh, but they had had a glorious day! I do wish I could manage breaks in the routine oftener. It gives them a new outlook on life and makes them more like normal children. Wasn't it really nice of Sandy? But you should have seen that man's behavior when I tried to thank him. He waved me aside in the middle of a sentence, and growlingly asked Miss Snaith if she couldn't economize a little on carbolic acid. The house smelt like a hospital.

I must tell you that Punch is back with us again, entirely renovated as to manners. I am looking for a family to adopt him. I had hoped those two intelligent spinsters would see their way to keeping him forever, but they want to travel, and they feel he's too consuming of their liberty. I enclose a sketch in colored chalk of your steamer, which he has just completed. There is some doubt as to the direction in which it is going; it looks as though it might progress backward and end in Brooklyn. Owing to the loss of my blue pencil, our flag has had to adopt the Italian colors.

The three figures on the bridge are you and Jervis and the baby. I am pained to note that you carry your daughter by the back of her neck, as if she were a kitten. That is not the way we handle babies in the J. G. H. nursery. Please also note that the artist has given Jervis his full due in the matter of legs. When I asked Punch what had

become of the captain, he said that the captain was inside, putting coal on the fire. Punch was terribly impressed, as well he might be, when he heard that your steamer burned three hundred wagon-loads a day, and he naturally supposed that all hands had been piped to the stoke-hole.

BOW! WOW!

That's a bark from Sing. I told him I was writing to you, and he responded instantly.

We both send love.

Yours,
SALLIE.

Dear Enemy:

You were so terribly gruff last night when I tried to thank you for giving my boys such a wonderful day that I didn't have a chance to express half of the appreciation I felt.

What on earth is the matter with you, Sandy? You used to be a tolerably nice man—in spots, but these last three or four months you have only been nice to other people, never to me.

We have had from the first a long series of misunderstandings and foolish contretemps, but after each one we seemed to reach a solider basis of understanding, until I had thought our friendship was on a pretty firm foundation, capable of withstanding any reasonable shock.

And then came that unfortunate evening last June when you overheard some foolish impolitenesses, which I did not in the slightest degree mean; and from then on you faded into the distance. Really, I have felt terribly bad about it, and have wanted to apologize, but your manner has not been inviting of confidence. It isn't that I have any excuse or explanation to offer; I haven't. You know how foolish and silly I am on occasions, but you will just have to realize that though I'm flippant and foolish and trivial on top, I am pretty solid inside; and you've got to forgive the silly part. The Pendletons knew that long ago, or they wouldn't have sent me up here. I have tried hard to pull off an honest job, partly because I wanted to justify their judgment, partly because I was really interested in

252

giving the poor little kiddies their share of happiness, but
mostly, I actually believe, because I wanted to show you
that your first derogatory opinion of me was ill founded.
Won't you please expunge that unfortunate fifteen minutes
at the porte-cochère last June, and remember instead the
fifteen hours I spent reading the Kallikak Family?

I would like to feel that we're friends again.

SALLIE MCBRIDE.

Dear Dr. MacRae:

I am in receipt of your calling card with an eleven-word answer to my letter on the back. I didn't mean to annoy you by my attentions. What you think and how you behave are really matters of extreme indifference to me. Be just as impolite as you choose.

S. McB.

December 14.

Dear Judy:

Please pepper your letters with stamps, inside and out. I
have thirty collectors in the family. Since you have taken
to travel, every day about post-time an eager group gathers
at the gate, waiting to snatch any letters of foreign design,
and by the time the letters reach me they are almost in
shreds through the tenacity of rival snatchers. Tell Jervis
to send us some more of those purple pine-trees from
Honduras; likewise some green parrots from Guatemala. I
could use a pint of them!

Isn't it wonderful to have got these apathetic little
things so enthusiastic? My children are getting to be almost like real children. B dormitory started a pillow-fight
last night of its own accord; and though it was very
wearing to our scant supply of linen, I stood by and
beamed, and even tossed a pillow myself.

Last Saturday those two desirable friends of Percy's spent
the whole afternoon playing with my boys. They brought
up three rifles, and each man took the lead of a camp of
Indians, and passed the afternoon in a bottle-shooting
contest, with a prize for the winning camp. They brought
the prize with them—an atrocious head of an Indian
painted on leather. Dreadful taste; but the men thought it
lovely, so I admired it with all the ardor I could assume.

When they had finished, I warmed them up with cookies and hot chocolate, and I really think the men enjoyed
it as much as the boys; they undoubtedly enjoyed it more
than I did. I couldn't help being in a feminine twitter all
the time the firing was going on for fear somebody would

shoot somebody else. But I know that I can't keep twenty-four Indians tied to my apron-strings, and I never could find in the whole wide world three nicer men to take an interest in them.

Just think of all that healthy, exuberant volunteer service going to waste under the asylum's nose! I suppose the neighborhood is full of plenty more of it, and I am going to make it my business to dig it out.

What I want most are about eight nice, pretty, sensible young women to come up here one night a week, and sit before the fire and tell stories while the chicks pop corn. I do so want to contrive a little individual petting for my babies. You see, Judy, I am remembering your own childhood, and am trying hard to fill in the gaps.

The trustees' meeting last week went beautifully. The new women are most helpful, and only the nice men came. I am happy to announce that the Hon. Cy Wykoff is visiting his married daughter in Scranton. I wish she would invite father to live with her permanently.

Wednesday.

I am in the most childish temper with the doctor, and for no very definite reason. He keeps along his even, unemotional way without paying the slightest attention to anything or anybody. I have swallowed more slights during these last few months than in the whole of my life before, and I'm developing the most shockingly revengeful nature. I spend all my spare time planning situations in which he will be terribly hurt and in need of my help, and in which I, with the utmost callousness, will shrug my shoulders and turn away. I am growing into a person entirely foreign to the sweet, sunny young thing you used to know.

Evening.

Do you realize that I am an authority on the care of dependent children? To-morrow I and other authorities visit officially the Hebrew Sheltering Guardian Society's Orphan Asylum at Pleasantville. (All that's its name!) It's a terribly difficult and roundabout journey from this point, involving a daybreak start and two trains and an automobile; but if I'm to be an authority, I must live up to the title. I'm keen about looking over other institutions and gleaning as many ideas as possible against our own alterations next year. And this Pleasantville asylum is an architectural model.

I acknowledge now, upon sober reflection, that we were wise to postpone extensive building operations until next summer. Of course I was disappointed, because it meant that I won't be the center of the ripping-up, and I do so love to be the center of ripping-ups! But, anyway, you'll take my advice, even though I'm no longer an official head? The two building details we did accomplish are very promising. Our new laundry grows better and better; it has removed from us that steamy smell so dear to asylums. The farmer's cottage will finally be ready for occupancy next week. All it now lacks is a coat of paint and some door-knobs.

But, oh dear! oh dear! another bubble has burst! Mrs. Turnfelt, for all her comfortable figure and sunny smile, hates to have children messing about. They make her nervous. And as for Turnfelt himself, though industrious and methodical and an excellent gardener, still, his mental processes are not quite what I had hoped for. When he first came, I made him free of the library. He began at the case nearest the door, which contains thirty-seven volumes of Pansy's works. Finally, after he had spent four months on Pansy, I suggested a change, and sent him home with "Huckleberry Finn." But he brought it back in a few days, and shook his head. He says that after reading Pansy, anything else seems tame. I am afraid I shall have to look about for some one a little more up-and-coming. But at least, compared with Sterry, Turnfelt is a scholar!

And speaking of Sterry, he paid us a social call a few days ago, in quite a chastened frame of mind. It seems that the "rich city feller" whose estate he has been managing no longer needs his services; and Sterry has graciously consented to return to us and let the children have gardens if they wish. I kindly, but convincingly, declined his offer.

Friday.

I came back from Pleasantville last night with a heart full of envy. Please, Mr. President, I want some gray stucco cottages, with Luca della Robbia figures baked into the front. They have nearly 700 children there, and all sizable youngsters. Of course that makes a very different problem from my hundred and seven, ranging from babyhood up. But I borrowed from their superintendent several very fancy ideas. I'm dividing my chicks into big and little sisters and brothers, each big one to have a little one to love and help and fight for. Big sister Sadie Kate has to see that little sister Gladiola always has her hair neatly combed and her stockings pulled up and knows her lessons and gets a touch of petting and her share of candy—very pleasant for Gladiola, but especially developing for Sadie Kate.

Also I am going to start among our older children a limited form of self-government such as we had in college. That will help fit them to go out into the world and govern themselves when they get there. This shoving children into the world at the age of sixteen seems terribly merciless. Five of my children are ready to be shoved, but I can't bring myself to do it. I keep remembering my own irresponsible silly young self, and wondering what would have happened to me had I been turned out to work at the age of sixteen!

I must leave you now to write an interesting letter to my politician in Washington, and it's hard work. What have I to say that will interest a politician? I can't do anything any more but babble about babies, and he wouldn't care if every baby was swept from the face of the earth. Oh, yes, he would, too! I'm afraid I'm slandering him. Babies—at least boy babies—grow into voters.

Good-by,
SALLIE.

Dearest Judy:

If you expect a cheerful letter from me the day, don't read this. The life of man is a wintry road. Fog, snow, rain, slush, drizzle, cold—such weather! such weather! And you in dear Jamaica with the sunshine and the orange-blossoms!

We've got whooping-cough, and you can hear us whoop when you get off the train two miles away. We don't know how we got it—just one of the pleasures of institution life. Cook has left,—in the night,—what the Scotch call a "moonlicht flitting." I don't know how she got her trunk away, but it's gone. The kitchen fire went with her. The pipes are frozen. The plumbers are here, and the kitchen floor is all ripped up. One of our horses has the spavin. And, to crown all, our cheery, resourceful Percy is down, down, down in the depths of despair. We have not been quite certain for three days past whether we could keep him from suicide. The girl in Detroit,—I knew she was a heartless little minx,—without so much as going through the formality of sending back his ring, has gone and married herself to a man and a couple of automobiles and a yacht. It is the best thing that could ever have happened to Percy, but it will be a long, long time before he realizes it.

We have our twenty-four Indians back in the house with us. I was sorry to have to bring them in, but the shacks were scarcely planned for winter quarters. I have stowed them away very comfortably, however, thanks to the spacious iron verandas surrounding our new fire-escape. It was a happy idea of Jervis's having them glassed in for sleeping-porches. The babies' sun-parlor is a wonderful

261

addition to our nursery. We can fairly see the little tots
bloom under the influence of that extra air and sunshine.

With the return of the Indians to civilized life, Percy's
occupation was ended, and he was supposed to remove
himself to the hotel. But he didn't want to remove himself. He has got used to orphans, he says, and he would
miss not seeing them about. I think the truth is that
he is feeling so miserable over his wrecked engagement
that he is afraid to be alone; he needs something to
occupy every waking moment out of banking hours. And
goodness knows we're glad enough to keep him! He has
been wonderful with those youngsters, and they need a
man's influence. But what on earth to do with the man?
As you discovered last summer, this spacious château does
not contain a superabundance of guest-rooms. He has
finally fitted himself into the doctor's laboratory, and the
medicines have moved themselves to a closet down the
hall. He and the doctor fixed it up between them, and if
they are willing to be mutually inconvenienced, I have no
fault to find.

Mercy! I've just looked at the calendar, and it's the
eighteenth, with Christmas only a week away. However
shall we finish all our plans in a week? The chicks are
making presents for one another, and something like a
thousand secrets have been whispered in my ear.

Snow last night. The boys have spent the morning in
the woods, gathering evergreens and drawing them home
on sleds; and twenty girls are spending the afternoon in
the laundry, winding wreaths for the windows. I don't
know how we are going to do our washing this week. We
were planning to keep the Christmas-tree a secret, but
fully fifty children have been boosted up to the carriage-

house window to take a peep at it, and I am afraid the
news has spread among the remaining fifty.

At your insistence, we have sedulously fostered the
Santa Claus myth, but it doesn't meet with much cre-
dence. "Why didn't he ever come before?" was Sadie
Kate's skeptical question. But Santa Claus is undoubtedly
coming this time. I asked the doctor, out of politeness, to
play the chief rôle at our Christmas-tree; and being certain
ahead of time that he was going to refuse, I had already
engaged Percy as an understudy. But there is no counting
on a Scotchman. Sandy accepted with unprecedented
graciousness, and I had privately to unengage Percy!

                                              Tuesday.

Isn't it funny, the way some inconsequential people
have of pouring out whatever happens to be churning
about in their minds at the moment? They seem to have
no residue of small talk, and are never able to dismiss a
crisis in order to discuss the weather.

This is apropos of a call I received to-day. A woman
had come to deliver her sister's child—sister in a sanatorium for tuberculosis; we to keep the child until the
mother is cured, though I fear, from what I hear, that will
never be. But, anyway, all the arrangements had been
made, and the woman had merely to hand in the little girl
and retire. But having a couple of hours between trains,
she intimated a desire to look about, so I showed her the
kindergarten-rooms and the little crib that Lily will occupy, and our yellow dining-room, with its frieze of bun-
nies, in order that she might report as many cheerful
details as possible to the poor mother. After this, as she

seemed tired, I socially asked her to walk into my parlor
and have a cup of tea. Doctor MacRae, being at hand and
in a hungry mood (a rare state for him; he now conde-
scends to a cup of tea with the officers of this institution
about twice a month), came, too, and we had a little
party.

The woman seemed to feel that the burden of entertainment rested upon her, and by way of making conversation, she told us that her husband had fallen in love
with the girl who sold tickets at a moving-picture show (a
painted, yellow-haired thing who chewed gum like a cow,
was her description of the enchantress), and he spent all
of his money on the girl, and never came home except
when he was drunk. Then he smashed the furniture something awful. An easel, with her mother's picture on it,
that she had had since before she was married, he had
thrown down just for the pleasure of hearing it crash. And
finally she had just got too tired to live, so she drank a
bottle of swamp-root because somebody had told her it was
poison if you took it all at once. But it didn't kill her; it
only made her sick. And he came back, and said he would
choke her if she ever tried that on him again; so she
guessed he must still care something for her. All this quite
casually while she stirred her tea.

I tried to think of something to say, but it was a social
exigency that left me dumb. But Sandy rose to the occasion like a gentleman. He talked to her beautifully and
sanely, and sent her away actually uplifted. Our Sandy,
when he tries, can be exceptionally nice, particularly to
people who have no claim upon him. I suppose it is a
matter of professional etiquette—part of a doctor's business to heal the spirit as well as the body. Most spirits

appear to need it in this world. My caller has left me needing it. I have been wondering ever since what I should do if I married a man who deserted me for a chewing-gum girl, and who came home and smashed the bric-à-brac. I suppose, judging from the theaters this winter, that it is a thing that might happen to any one, particularly in the best sociey.

You ought to be thankful you've got Jervis. There is something awfully certain about a man like him. The longer I live, the surer I am that character is the only thing that counts. But how on earth can you ever tell? Men are so good at talking!

Good-by, and a merry Christmas to Jervis and both Judies.

S. McB.

P.S. It would be a pleasant attention if you would answer my letters a little more promptly.

Dear Judy:

Sadie Kate has spent the week composing a Christmas letter to you, and it leaves nothing for me to tell. Oh, we've had a wonderful time! Besides all the presents and games and fancy things to eat, we have had hay-rides and skating-parties and candy-pulls. I don't know whether these pampered little orphans will ever settle down again into normal children.

Many thanks for my six gifts. I like them all, particularly the picture of Judy, Junior; the tooth adds a pleasant touch to her smile.

You'll be glad to hear that I've placed out Hattie Heaphy in a minister's family, and a dear family they are; they never blinked an eyelash when I told them about the communion-cup. They've given her to themselves for a Christmas present, and she went off so happily, clinging to her new father's hand!

I won't write more now, because fifty children are writing thank-you letters, and poor Aunt Judy will be buried beneath her mail when this week's steamer gets in.

My love to the Pendletons.

S. McB.

P.S. Singapore sends his love to Togo, and is sorry he bit him on the ear.

O, dear, Gordon, I have been reading the most upsetting book!

I tried to talk some French the other day, and not
making out very well, decided that I had better take my
French in hand if I didn't want to lose it entirely. That
Scotch doctor of ours has mercifully abandoned my scientific education, so I have a little time at my own disposal.
By some unlucky chance I began with "Numa Roumestan,"
by Daudet. It is a terribly disturbing book for a girl to read
who is engaged to a politician. Read it, Gordon dear, and
assiduously train your character away from Numa's. It's the
story of a politician who is disquietingly fascinating (like
you). Who is adored by all who know him (like you). Who
has a most persuasive way of talking and makes wonderful
speeches (again like you). He is worshiped by everybody,
and they all say to his wife, "What a happy life you must
lead, knowing so intimately that wonderful man!"

But he wasn't very wonderful when he came home to
her—only when he had an audience and applause. He
would drink with every casual acquaintance, and be gay
and bubbling and expansive; and then return morose and
sullen and down. "Joie de rue, douleur de maison," is the
burden of the book.

I read it till twelve last night, and honestly I didn't
sleep for being scared. I know you'll be angry, but really
and truly, Gordon dear, there's just a touch too much
truth in it for my entire amusement. I didn't mean even
to refer again to that unhappy matter of August 20,—we

talked it all out at the time,—but you know perfectly that you need a bit of watching. And I don't like the idea. I want to have a feeling of absolute confidence and stability about the man I marry. I never could live in a state of anxious waiting for him to come home.

Read "Numa" for yourself, and you'll see the woman's point of view. I'm not patient or meek or long-suffering in any way, and I'm a little afraid of what I'm capable of doing if I have the provocation. My heart has to be in a thing in order to make it work, and, oh, I do so want our marriage to work!

Please forgive me for writing all this. I don't mean that I really think you'll be a "joy of the street, and sorrow of the home." It's just that I didn't sleep last night, and I feel sort of hollow behind the eyes.

May the year that's coming bring good counsel and happiness and tranquillity to both of us!

As ever,
S.

January 1.

Dear Judy:

Something terribly sort of queer has happened, and positively I don't know whether it did happen or whether I dreamed it. I'll tell you from the beginning, and I think it might be as well if you burned this letter; it's not quite proper for Jervis's eyes.

You remember my telling you the case of Thomas Kehoe, whom we placed out last June? He had an alcoholic heredity on both sides, and as a baby seems to have been fattened on beer instead of milk. He entered the John Grier at the age of nine, and twice, according to his record in the Doomsday Book, he managed to get himself intoxicated, once on beer stolen from some workmen, and once (and thoroughly) on cooking brandy. You can see with what misgivings we placed him out; but we warned the family (hardworking temperate farming-people) and hoped for the best.

Yesterday the family telegraphed that they could keep him no longer. Would I please meet him on the six o'clock train? Turnfelt met the six o'clock train. No boy. I sent a night message telling of his nonarrival and asking for particulars.

I stayed up later than usual last night putting my desk in order and—sort of making up my mind to face the New Year. Toward twelve I suddenly realized that the hour was late and that I was very tired. I had begun getting ready for bed when I was startled by a banging on the front door. I stuck my head out of the window and demanded who was there.

"Tommy Kehoe," said a very shaky voice.

I went down and opened the door, and that lad, sixteen years old, tumbled in, dead drunk. Thank Heaven! Percy Witherspoon was within call, and not away off in the Indian camp. I roused him, and together we conveyed Thomas to our guest-room, the only decently isolated spot in the building. Then I telephoned for the doctor, who, I am afraid, had already had a long day. He came, and we put in a pretty terrible night. It developed afterward that the boy had brought along with his luggage a bottle of liniment belonging to his employer. It was made half of alcohol and half of witch-hazel; and Thomas had refreshed his journey with this!

He was in such shape that positively I didn't think we'd pull him through—and I hoped we wouldn't. If I were a physician, I'd let such cases gently slip away for the good of society; but you should have seen Sandy work! That terrible life-saving instinct of his was aroused, and he fought with every inch of energy he possessed.

I made black coffee, and helped all I could, but the details were pretty messy, and I left the two men to deal with him alone and went back to my room. But I didn't attempt to go to bed; I was afraid they might be wanting me again. Toward four o'clock Sandy came to my library with word that the boy was asleep and that Percy had moved up a cot and would sleep in his room the rest of the night. Poor Sandy looked sort of ashen and haggard and done with life. As I looked at him, I thought about how desperately he worked to save others, and never saved himself, and about that dismal home of his, with never a touch of cheer, and the horrible tragedy in the background of his life. All the rancor I've been saving up seemed to vanish, and a wave of sympathy swept over me. I stretched my hand out to him; he stretched his out to me. And suddenly—I don't know—something electric happened. In another moment we were in each other's arms. He loosened my hands, and put me down in the big arm-chair. "My God! Sallie, do you think I'm made of iron?" he said and walked out. I went to sleep in the chair, and when I woke the sun was shining in my eyes and Jane was standing over me in amazed consternation.

This morning at eleven he came back, looked me coldly in the eye without so much as the flicker of an eyelash, and told me that Thomas was to have hot milk every two hours and that the spots in Maggie Peters's throat must be watched.

Here we are back on our old standing, and positively I don't know but what I dreamed that one minute in the night!

But it would be a piquant situation, wouldn't it, if Sandy and I should discover that we were falling in love with each other, he with a perfectly good wife in the insane asylum and I with an outraged fiancé in Washington? I don't know but what the wisest thing for me to do is to resign at once and take myself home, where I can placidly settle down to a few months of embroidering "S McB" on table-cloths, like any other respectable engaged girl.

I repeat very firmly that this letter isn't for Jervis's consumption. Tear it into little pieces and scatter them in the Caribbean.

S.

Dear Gordon:

You are right to be annoyed. I know I'm not a satisfactory love-letter writer. I have only to glance at the published correspondence of Elizabeth Barrett and Robert Browning to realize that the warmth of my style is not up to standard. But you know already—you have known a long time—that I am not a very emotional person. I suppose I might write a lot of such things as: "Every waking moment you are in my thoughts." "My dear boy, I only live when you are near." But it wouldn't be absolutely true. You don't fill all my thoughts; 107 orphans do that. And I really am quite comfortably alive whether you are here or not. I have to be natural. You surely don't want me to pretend more desolation than I feel. But I do love to see you,—you know that perfectly,—and I am disappointed when you can't come. I fully appreciate all your charming qualities, but, my dear boy, I *can't* be sentimental on paper. I am always thinking about the hotel chambermaid who reads the letters you casually leave on your bureau. You needn't expostulate that you carry them next your heart, for I know perfectly well that you don't.

Forgive me for that last letter if it hurt your feelings. Since I came to this asylum I am extremely touchy on the subject of drink; you would be, too, if you had seen what I have seen. Several of my chicks are the sad result of alcoholic parents, and they are never going to have a fair chance all their lives. You can't look about a place like this without "aye keeping up a terrible thinking."

272

You are right, I am afraid, about it's being a woman's trick to make a great show of forgiving a man, and then never letting him hear the end of it. Well, Gordon, I positively don't know what the word "forgiving" means. It can't include "forgetting," for that is a physiological process, and does not result from an act of the will. We all have a collection of memories that we would happily lose, but somehow those are just the ones that insist upon sticking. If "forgiving" means promising never to speak of a thing again, I can doubtless manage that. But it isn't always the wisest way to shut an unpleasant memory inside you. It grows and grows, and runs all through you like a poison.

Oh dear! I really didn't mean to be saying all this. I try to be the cheerful, care-free (and somewhat light-headed) Sallie you like best; but I've come in touch with a great deal of *realness* during this last year, and I'm afraid I've grown into a very different person from the girl you fell in love with. I'm no longer a gay young thing playing with life. I know it pretty thoroughly now, and that means that I can't be always laughing.

I know this is another beastly uncheerful letter,—as bad as the last, and maybe worse,—but if you knew what we've just been through! A boy—sixteen—of unspeakable heredity has nearly poisoned himself with a disgusting mixture of alcohol and witch-hazel. We have been working three days over him, and are just sure now that he is going to recuperate sufficiently to do it again! "It's a gude warld, but they're ill that's in't."

Please excuse that Scotch—it slipped out. Please excuse everything.

SALLIE.

Dear Judy:

I hope my two cablegrams didn't give you too terrible a shock. I would have waited to let the first news come by letter, with a chance for details, but I was so afraid you might hear it in some indirect way. The whole thing is dreadful enough, but no lives were lost, and only one serious accident. We can't help shuddering at the thought of how much worse it might have been, with over a hundred sleeping children in this fire-trap of a building. That new fire-escape was absolutely useless. The wind was blowing toward it, and the flames simply enveloped it. We saved them all by the center stairs—but I'll begin at the beginning, and tell the whole story.

It had rained all day Friday, thanks to a merciful Providence, and the roofs were thoroughly soaked. Toward night it began to freeze, and the rain turned to sleet. By ten o'clock, when I went to bed, the wind was blowing a terrible gale from the northwest, and everything loose about the building was banging and rattling. About two o'clock I suddenly started wide awake, with a bright light in my eyes. I jumped out of bed and ran to the window. The carriage-house was a mass of flames, and a shower of sparks was sweeping over our eastern wing. I ran to the bathroom and leaned out of the window. I could see that the roof over the nursery was already blazing in half a dozen places.

Well, my dear, my heart just simply didn't beat for as much as a minute. I thought of those seventeen babies up under that roof, and I couldn't swallow. I finally managed

274

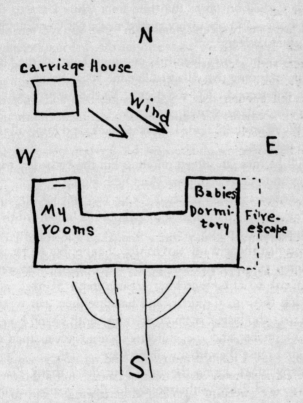

to get my shaking knees to work again, and I dashed back to the hall, grabbing my automobile coat as I ran.

I drummed on Betsy's and Miss Matthews' and Miss Snaith's doors, just as Mr. Witherspoon, who had also been wakened by the light, came tumbling upstairs three steps at a time, struggling into an overcoat as he ran.

"Get all the children down to the dining-room, babies first," I gasped. "I'll turn in the alarm."

He dashed on up to the third floor while I ran to the telephone—and oh, I thought I'd never get Central! She was sound asleep.

"The John Grier Home is burning! Turn in the fire-alarm and rouse the village. Give me 505," I said.

In one second I had the doctor. Maybe I wasn't glad to hear his cool, unexcited voice!

"We're on fire!" I cried. "Come quick, and bring all the men you can!"

"I'll be there in fifteen minutes. Fill the bath-tubs with water and put in blankets." And he hung up.

I dashed back to the hall. Betsy was ringing our fire-bell, and Percy had already routed out his Indian tribes in dormitories B and C.

Our first thought was not to stop the fire, but to get the children to a place of safety. We began in G, and went from crib to crib, snatching a baby and a blanket, and rushing them to the door, and handing them out to the Indians, who lugged them down-stairs. Both G and F were full of smoke, and the children so dead asleep that we couldn't rouse them to a walking state.

Many times during the next hour did I thank Providence—and Percy Witherspoon—for those vociferous fire-drills we have suffered weekly. The twenty-four oldest boys, under his direction, never lost their heads for a second. They divided into four tribes, and sprang to their posts like little soldiers. Two tribes helped in the work of clearing the dormitories and keeping the terrified children in order. One tribe worked the hose from the cupola tank until the firemen came, and the rest devoted themselves to salvage. They spread sheets on the floor, dumped the contents of lockers and bureau drawers into them, and bundled them down the stairs. All of the extra clothes were saved except those the children had actually been wearing the day before, and most of the staff's things. But clothes, bedding—everything belonging to G and F went. The rooms were too full of smoke to make it safe to enter after we had got out the last child.

By the time the doctor arrived with Luellen and two neighbors he had picked up, we were marching the last dormitory down to the kitchen, the most remote corner from the fire. The poor chicks were mainly bare-footed and wrapped in blankets; we told them to bring their clothes when we wakened them, but in their fright they thought only of getting out.

By this time the halls were so full of smoke we could scarcely breathe. It looked as though the whole building would go, though the wind was blowing away from my west wing.

Another automobile full of retainers from Knowltop came up almost immediately, and they all fell to fighting the fire. The regular fire department didn't come for ten minutes after that. You see, they have only horses, and we are three miles out, and the roads pretty bad. It was a dreadful night, cold and sleety, and such a wind blowing that you could scarcely stand up. The men climbed out on the roof, and worked in their stocking-feet to keep from slipping off. They beat out the sparks with wet blankets, and chopped, and squirted that tankful of water, and behaved like heroes.

The doctor meanwhile took charge of the children. Our first thought was to get them away to a place of safety, for if the whole building should go, we couldn't march them out of doors into that awful wind, with only their nightclothes and blankets for protection. By this time several more automobiles full of men had come, and we requisitioned the cars.

Knowltop had providentially been opened for the weekend in order to entertain a house-party in honor of the old gentleman's sixty-seventh birthday. He was one of the first to arrive, and he put his entire place at our disposal. It was the nearest refuge, and we accepted it instantaneously. We bundled our twenty littlest tots into cars, and ran them down to the house. The guests, who were excitedly dressing in order to come to the fire, received the chicks and tucked them away into their own beds. This pretty well filled up all the available house room, but Mr. Reimer (Mr. Knowltop's family name) has just built a big new stucco barn, with a garage hitched to it, all nicely heated, and ready for us.

After the babies were disposed of in the house, those helpful guests got to work and fixed the barn to receive the next older kiddies. They covered the floor with hay, and spread blankets and carriage robes over it, and bedded down thirty of the children in rows like little calves. Miss Matthews and a nurse went with them, administered hot milk all around, and within half an hour the tots were sleeping as peacefully as in their little cribs.

But meanwhile we at the house were having sensations. The doctor's first question upon arrival had been:

"You've counted the children? You know they're all here?"

"We've made certain that every dormitory was empty before we left it," I replied.

You see, they couldn't be counted in that confusion; twenty or so of the boys were still in the dormitories, working under Percy Witherspoon to save clothing and furniture, and the older girls were sorting over bushels of shoes and trying to fit them to the little ones, who were running about underfoot and wailing dismally.

Well, after we had loaded and despatched about seven car-loads of children, the doctor suddenly called out:

"Where's Allegra?"

There was a horrified silence. No one had seen her. And then Miss Snaith stood up and *shrieked*. Betsy took her by the shoulders, and shook her into coherence.

It seems that she had thought Allegra was coming down with a cough, and in order to get her out of the cold, had moved her crib from the fresh-air nursery into the store-room—and then forgotten it.

Well, my dear, you know where the store-room is! We simply stared at one another with white faces. By this time the whole east wing was gutted and the third-floor stairs in flames. There didn't seem a chance that the child was still alive. The doctor was the first to move. He snatched up a wet blanket that was lying in a soppy pile on the floor of the hall and sprang for the stairs. We yelled to him to come back. It simply looked like suicide; but he kept on, and disappeared into the smoke. I dashed outside and shouted to the firemen on the roof. The store-room window was too little for a man to go through, and they hadn't opened it for fear of creating a draft.

I can't describe what happened in the next agonizing ten minutes. The third-floor stairs fell in with a crash and a burst of flame about five seconds after the doctor passed over them. We had given him up for lost when a shout

went up from the crowd on the lawn, and he appeared for
an instant at one of those dormer-windows in the attic,
and called for the firemen to put up a ladder. Then he
disappeared, and it seemed to us that they'd never get that
ladder in place; but they finally did, and two men went
up. The opening of the window had created a draft, and
they were almost overpowered by the volume of smoke
that burst out at the top. After an eternity the doctor
appeared again with a white bundle in his arms. He passed
it out to the men, and then he staggered back and dropped
out of sight!

I don't know what happened for the next few minutes; I
turned away and shut my eyes. Somehow or other they got
him out and half-way down the ladder, and then they let
him slip. You see, he was unconscious from all the smoke
he'd swallowed, and the ladder was slippery with ice and
terribly wobbly. Anyway, when I looked again he was
lying in a heap on the ground, with the crowd all running,
and somebody yelling to give him air. They thought at
first he was dead. But Dr. Metcalf from the village examined him, and said his leg was broken, and two ribs, and
that aside from that he seemed whole. He was still unconscious when they put him on two of the baby mattresses
that had been thrown out of the windows and laid him in
the wagon that brought the ladders and started him home.

And the rest of us, left behind, kept right on with the
work as though nothing had happened. The queer thing
about a calamity like this is that there is so much to be
done on every side that you don't have a moment to think,
and you don't get any of your values straightened out until
afterward. The doctor, without a moment's hesitation,
had risked his life to save Allegra. It was the bravest thing

I ever saw, and yet the whole business occupied only fifteen minutes out of that dreadful night. At the time, it was just an incident.

And he saved Allegra. She came out of that blanket with rumpled hair and a look of pleased surprise at the new game of peek-a-boo. She was smiling! The child's escape was little short of a miracle. The fire had started within three feet of her wall, but owing to the direction of the wind, it had worked away from her. If Miss Snaith had believed a little more in fresh air and had left the window open, the fire would have eaten back; but fortunately Miss Snaith does not believe in fresh air, and no such thing happened. If Allegra had gone, I never should have forgiven myself for not letting the Bretlands take her, and I know that Sandy wouldn't.

Despite all the loss, I can't be anything but happy when I think of the two horrible tragedies that have been averted; for seven minutes, while the doctor was penned in that blazing third floor, I lived through the agony of believing them both gone, and I start awake in the night trembling with horror.

But I'll try to tell you the rest. The firemen and the volunteers—particularly the chauffeur and stablemen from Knowltop—worked all night in an absolute frenzy. Our newest negro cook, who is a heroine in her own right, went out and started the laundry fire and made up a boilerful of coffee. It was her own idea. The non-combatants served it to the firemen when they relieved one another for a few minutes' rest, and it helped.

We got the remainder of the children off to various hospitable houses, except the older boys, who worked all night as well as any one. It was absolutely inspiring to see the way this entire township turned out and helped. People who haven't appeared to know that the asylum existed came in the middle of the night and put their whole houses at our disposal. They took the children in, gave them hot baths and hot soup, and tucked them into bed. And so far as I can make out, not one of my one hundred and seven chicks is any the worse for hopping about on drenched floors in their bare feet, not even the whooping-cough cases.

It was broad daylight before the fire was sufficiently under control to let us know just what we had saved. I will report that my wing is entirely intact, though a little smoky, and the main corridor is pretty nearly all right up to the center staircase; after that everything is charred and drenched. The east wing is a blackened, roofless shell. Your hated Ward F, dear Judy, is gone forever. I wish that you could obliterate it from your mind as absolutely as it is obliterated from the earth. Both in substance and in spirit the old John Grier is done for.

I must tell you something funny; I never saw so many funny things in my life as happened through that night. When everybody there was in extreme negligée, most of the men in pajamas and ulsters, and all of them without collars, the Hon. Cyrus Wykoff put in a tardy appearance, arrayed as for an afternoon tea. He wore a pearl scarf-pin and white spats! But he really was extremely helpful. He put his entire house at our disposal, and I turned over to him Miss Snaith in a state of hysterics, and her nerves so fully occupied him that he didn't get in our way the whole night through.

I can't write any more details now; I've never been so rushed in the whole of my life. I'll just assure you that there's no slightest reason for you to cut your trip short. Five trustees were on the spot early Saturday morning, and we are all working like mad to get affairs into some semblance of order. Our asylum at the present moment is scattered over the entire township; but don't be unduly anxious. We know where all the children are. None of them is permanently mislaid. I didn't know that perfect strangers could be so kind. My opinion of the human race has gone up.

I haven't seen the doctor. They telegraphed to New York for a surgeon, who set his leg. The break was pretty bad, and will take time; they don't think there are any internal injuries, though he is awfully battered up. As soon as we are allowed to see him I will send more detailed particulars. I really must stop if I am to catch to-morrow's steamer.

Good-by. Don't worry. There are a dozen silver linings to this cloud that I'll write about to-morrow.

SALLIE.

Good heavens! here comes an automobile with J. F. Bretland in it!

Dear Judy:

Listen to this! J. F. Bretland read about our fire in a New York paper (I will say that the metropolitan press made the most of details), and he posted up here in a twitter of anxiety. His first question as he tumbled across our blackened threshold was, "Is Allegra safe?"

"Yes," said I.

"Thank God!" he cried, and dropped into a chair. "This is no place for children," he said severely, "and I have come to take her home. I want the boys, too," he added hastily before I had a chance to speak. "My wife and I have talked it over, and we have decided that since we are going to the trouble of starting a nursery, we might as well run it for three as for one."

I led him up to my library, where our little family has been domiciled since the fire, and ten minutes later, when I was called down to confer with the trustees, I left J. F. Bretland with his new daughter on his knee and a son leaning against each arm, the proudest father in the United States.

So, you see, our fire has accomplished one thing: those three children are settled for life. It is almost worth the loss.

But I don't believe I told you how the fire started. There are so many things I haven't told you that my arm aches at the thought of writing them all. Sterry, we have since discovered, was spending the week-end as our guest. After a bibulous evening passed at "Jack's Place," he

284

returned to our carriage-house, climbed in through a window, lighted a candle, made himself comfortable, and dropped asleep. He must have forgotten to put out the candle; anyway, the fire happened, and Sterry just escaped with his life. He is now in the town hospital, bathed in sweet-oil, and painfully regretting his share in our troubles.

I am pleased to learn that our insurance was pretty adequate, so the money loss won't be so tremendous, after all. As for other kinds of loss, there aren't any! Actually, nothing but gain so far as I can make out, barring, of course, our poor smashed-up doctor. Everybody has been wonderful; I didn't know that so much charity and kindness existed in the human race. Did I ever say anything against trustees? I take it back. Four of them posted up from New York the morning after the fire, and all of the local people have been wonderful. Even the Hon. Cy has been so occupied in remarking the morals of the five orphans quartered upon him that he hasn't caused any trouble at all.

The fire occurred early Saturday morning, and Sunday the ministers in all the churches called for volunteers to accept in their houses one or two children as guests for three weeks, until the asylum could get its plant into working order again.

It was inspiring to see the response. Every child was disposed of within half an hour. And consider what that means for the future: every one of those families is going to take a personal interest in this asylum from now on. Also, consider what it means for the children. They are finding out how a real family lives, and this is the first time that dozens of them have ever crossed the threshold of a private house.

As for more permanent plans to take us through the winter, listen to all this. The country club has a caddies' club-house which they don't use in winter and which they have politely put at our disposal. It joins our land on the back, and we are fitting it up for fourteen children, with Miss Matthews in charge. Our dining-room and kitchen still being intact, they will come here for meals and school, returning home at night all the better for half a mile walk. "The Pavilion on the Links" we are calling it.

Then that nice motherly Mrs. Wilson, next door to the doctor's,—she who has been so efficient with our little Loretta,—has agreed to take in five more at four dollars a week each. I am leaving with her some of the most promising older girls who have shown housekeeping instincts, and would like to learn cooking on a decently small scale. Mrs. Wilson and her husband are such a wonderful couple, thrifty and industrious and simple and loving, I think it would do the girls good to observe them. A training class in wifehood!

I told you about the Knowltop people on the east of us, who took in forty-seven youngsters the night of the fire, and how their entire house-party turned themselves into emergency nurse-maids? We relieved them of thirty-six the next day, but they still have eleven. Did I ever call Mr. Knowltop a crusty old curmudgeon? I take it back. I beg his pardon. He's a sweet lamb. Now, in the time of our need, what do you think that blessed man has done? He has fitted up an empty tenant house on the estate for our babies, has himself engaged an English trained baby-nurse to take charge, and furnishes them with the superior milk from his own model dairy. He says he has been wondering

for years what to do with that milk. He can't afford to sell
it, because he loses four cents on every quart!

The twelve older girls from dormitory A I am putting
into the farmer's new cottage; the poor Turnfelts, who had
occupied it just two days, are being shoved on into the
village. But they wouldn't be any good in looking after
the children, and I need their room. Three or four of
these girls have been returned from foster-homes as intrac-
table, and they require pretty efficient supervision. So
what do you think I've done? Telegraphed to Helen Brooks
to chuck the publishers and take charge of my girls instead. You know she will be wonderful with them. She
accepted provisionally. Poor Helen has had enough of this
irrevocable contract business; she wants everything in life
to be on trial!

For the older boys something particularly nice has happened; we have received a gift of gratitude from J. F.
Bretland. He went down to thank the doctor for Allegra;
they had a long talk about the needs of the institution,
and J. F. B. came back and gave me a check for $3,000 to
build the Indian camps on a substantial scale. He and Percy
and the village architect have drawn up plans, and in two
weeks, we hope, the tribes will move into winter quarters.

What does it matter if my one hundred and seven
children have been burned out, since they live in such a
kind-hearted world as this?

Friday.

I suppose you are wondering why I don't vouchsafe
some details about the doctor's condition. I can't give any
first-hand information, since he won't see me. However,

he has seen everybody except me—Betsy, Allegra, Mrs.
Livermore, Mr. Bretland, Percy, various trustees; they all
report that he is progressing as comfortably as could be
expected with two broken ribs and a fractured fibula.
That, I believe, is the professional name of the particular
leg bone he broke. He doesn't like to have a fuss made
over him, and he won't pose gracefully as a hero. I myself,
as grateful head of this institution, called on several different occasions to present my official thanks, but I was
invariably met at the door with word that he was sleeping
and did not wish to be disturbed. The first two times I
believed Mrs. McGurk; after that—well, I know our doctor! So when it came time to send our little maid to
prattle her unconscious good-bys to the man who had
saved her life, I despatched her in charge of Betsy.

I haven't an idea what is the matter with the man. He
was friendly enough last week, but now, if I want an
opinion from him, I have to send Percy to extract it. I do
think that he might see me as the superintendent of the
asylum, even if he doesn't wish our acquaintance to be on
a personal basis. There is no doubt about it, our Sandy is
Scotch!

LATER.

It is going to require a fortune in stamps to get this
letter to Jamaica, but I do want you to know all the news,
and we have never had so many exhilarating things happen since 1876, when we were founded. This fire has
given us such a shock that we are going to be more alive
for years to come. I believe that every institution ought to
be burned to the ground every twenty-five years in order to

get rid of old-fashioned equipment and obsolete ideas. I am superlatively glad now that we didn't spend Jervis's money last summer; it would have been intensively tragic to have had that burn. I don't mind so much about John Grier's, since he made it in a patent medicine which, I hear, contained opium.

As to the remnant of us that the fire left behind, it is already boarded up and covered with tar-paper, and we are living along quite comfortably in our portion of a house. It affords sufficient room for the staff and the children's dining-room and kitchen, and more permanent plans can be made later.

Do you perceive what has happened to us? The good Lord has heard my prayer, and the John Grier Home is a cottage institution!

I am,

The busiest person north of the equator,

S. McBRIDE.

Dear Gordon:

Please, please behave yourself, and don't make things harder than they are. It's absolutely out of the question for me to give up the asylum this instant. You ought to realize that I can't abandon my chicks just when they are so terribly in need of me. Neither am I ready to drop this blasted philanthropy. (You can see how your language looks in my handwriting!)

You have no cause to worry. I am not overworking. I am enjoying it; never was so busy and happy in my life. The papers made the fire out much more lurid than it really was. That picture of me leaping from the roof with a baby under each arm was overdrawn. One or two of the children have sore throats, and our poor doctor is in a plaster cast; but we're alive, thank Heaven! and are going to pull through without permanent scars.

I can't write details now; I'm simply rushed to death. And don't come—please! Later, when things have settled just a little, you and I must have a talk about you and me, but I want time to think about it first.

S.

January 21.

Dear Judy:

Helen Brooks is taking hold of those fourteen fractious girls in a most masterly fashion. The job is quite the toughest I had to offer, and she likes it. I think she is going to be a valuable addition to our staff.

And I forgot to tell you about Punch. When the fire occurred, those two nice women who kept him all summer were on the point of catching a train for California—and they simply tucked him under their arms, along with their luggage, and carried him off. So Punch spends the winter in Pasadena, and I rather fancy he is theirs for good. Do you wonder that I am in an exalted mood over all these happenings?

LATER.

Poor bereaved Percy has just been spending the evening with me, because I am supposed to understand his troubles. Why must I be supposed to understand everybody's troubles? It's awfully wearing to be pouring out sympathy from an empty heart. The poor boy at present is pretty low, but I rather suspect—with Betsy's aid—that he will pull through. He is just on the edge of falling in love with Betsy, but he doesn't know it. He's in the stage now where he's sort of enjoying his troubles; he feels himself a tragic hero, a man who has suffered deeply. But I notice that when Betsy is about, he offers cheerful assistance in whatever work is toward.

Gordon telegraphed to-day that he is coming to-mor-

row. I am dreading the interview, for I know we are going
to have an altercation. He wrote the day after the fire and
begged me to "chuck the asylum" and get married immediately, and now he's coming to argue it out. I can't make
him understand that a job involving the happiness of one
hundred or so children can't be chucked with such charming insouciance. I tried my best to keep him away, but,
like the rest of his sex, he's stubborn. Oh dear, I don't
know what's ahead of us! I wish I could glance into next
year for a moment.

The doctor is still in his plaster cast, but I hear is doing
well, after a grumbly fashion. He is able to sit up a little
every day and to receive a carefully selected list of visitors.
Mrs. McGurk sorts them out at the door, and repudiates
the ones she doesn't like.

Good-by. I'd write some more, but I'm so sleepy that
my eyes are shutting on me. (The idiom is Sadie Kate's.) I
must go to bed and get some sleep against the one hundred and seven troubles of to-morrow.

With love to the Pendletons,

                                          S. McB.

Dear Judy:

This letter has nothing to do with the John Grier Home. It's merely from Sallie McBride.

Do you remember when we read Huxley's letters our senior year? That book contained a phrase which has stuck in my memory ever since: "There is always a Cape Horn in one's life that one either weathers or wrecks oneself on." It's terribly true; and the trouble is that you can't always recognize your Cape Horn when you see it. The sailing is sometimes pretty foggy, and you're wrecked before you know it.

I've been realizing of late that I have reached the Cape Horn of my own life. I entered upon my engagement to Gordon honestly and hopefully, but little by little I've grown doubtful of the outcome. The girl he loves is not the *me* I want to be. It's the *me* I've been trying to grow away from all this last year. I'm not sure she ever really existed. Gordon just imagined she did. Anyway, she doesn't exist any more, and the only fair course both to him and to myself was to end it.

We no longer have any interests in common; we are not friends. He doesn't comprehend it; he thinks that I am making it up, that all I have to do is to take an interest in his life, and everything will turn out happily. Of course I do take an interest when he's with me. I talk about the things he wants to talk about, and he doesn't know that there's a whole part of me—the biggest part of me—that simply doesn't meet him at any point. I pretend when I am with him. I am not myself, and if we were to live

293

together in constant daily intercourse, I'd have to keep on pretending all my life. He wants me to watch his face and smile when he smiles and frown when he frowns. He can't realize that I'm an individual just as much as he is.

I have social accomplishments. I dress well, I'm spectacular, I would be an ideal hostess in a politician's household— and that's why he likes me.

Anyway, I suddenly saw with awful distinctness that if I kept on I'd be in a few years where Helen Brooks is. She's a far better model of married life for me to contemplate just this moment than you, dear Judy. I think that such a spectacle as you and Jervis are a menace to society. You look so happy and peaceful and companionable that you induce a defenseless on-looker to rush off and snap up the first man she meets—and he's always the wrong man.

Anyway, Gordon and I have quarreled definitely and finally. I should rather have ended without a quarrel, but considering his temperament,—and mine, too, I must confess,—we had to go off in a big smoky explosion. He came yesterday afternoon, after I'd written him not to come, and we went walking over Knowltop. For three and a half hours we paced back and forth over that windy moor and discussed ourselves to the bottommost recesses of our beings. No one can ever say the break came through misunderstanding each other!

It ended by Gordon's going, never to return. As I stood there at the end and watched him drop out of sight over the brow of the hill, and realized that I was free and alone and my own master, well, Judy, such a sense of joyous relief, of freedom, swept over me! I can't tell you; I don't believe any happily married person could ever realize how wonderfully, beautifully *alone* I felt. I wanted to throw my

arms out and embrace the whole waiting world that be-
longed suddenly to me. Oh, it is such a relief to have it
settled! I faced the truth the night of the fire when I saw
the old John Grier go, and realized that a new John Grier
would be built in its place and that I wouldn't be here to
do it. A horrible jealousy clutched at my heart. I couldn't
give it up, and during those agonizing moments while I
thought we had lost our doctor, I realized what his life
meant, and how much more significant than Gordon's.
And I knew then that I couldn't desert him; I had to go
on and carry out all of the plans we made together.

I don't seem to be telling you anything but a mess of
words, I am so full of such a mess of crowding emotions; I
want to talk and talk and talk myself into coherence.
But, anyway, I stood alone in the winter twilight, and
I took a deep breath of clear cold air, and I felt beautifully, wonderfully, electrically free; and then I ran and
leaped and skipped down the hill and across the pastures
toward our iron confines, and I sang to myself. Oh, it
was a scandalous proceeding, when, according to all
precedent, I should have gone trailing home with a
broken wing. I never gave one thought to poor Gordon,
who was carrying a broken, bruised, betrayed heart to the
railroad station.

As I entered the house I was greeted by the joyous
clatter of the children trooping to their supper. They were
suddenly *mine*, and lately, as my doom became more and
more imminent, they had seemed fading away into little
strangers. I seized the three nearest and hugged them
hard. I have suddenly found such new life and exuber-
ance, I feel as though I had been released from prison and
were free. I feel,—oh, I'll stop,—I just want you to know

the truth. Don't show Jervis this letter, but tell him what's in it in a decently subdued and mournful fashion.

It's midnight now, and I'm going to try to go to sleep. It's wonderful not to be going to marry some one you don't want to marry. I'm glad of all these children's needs, I'm glad of Helen Brooks, and, yes, of the fire, and everything that has made me see clearly. There's never been a divorce in my family, and they would have hated it.

I know I'm horribly egotistical and selfish; I ought to be thinking of poor Gordon's broken heart. But really it would just be a pose if I pretended to be very sorrowful. He'll find some one else with just as conspicuous hair as mine, who will make just as effective a hostess, and who won't be bothered by any of these damned modern ideas about public service and woman's mission and all the rest of the tomfoolery the modern generation of women is addicted to. (I paraphrase, and soften our young man's heartbroken utterances.)

Good-by, dear people. How I wish I could stand with you on your beach and look across the blue, blue sea! I salute the Spanish main.

Addio!
SALLIE

January 27.

Dear Dr. MacRae:

I wonder if this note will be so fortunate as to find you awake? Perhaps you are not aware that I have called four times to offer thanks and consolation in my best bed-side manner? I am touched by the news that Mrs. McGurk's time is entirely occupied in taking in flowers and jelly and chicken broth, donated by the adoring ladies of the parish to the ungracious hero in a plaster cast. I know that you find a cap of homespun more comfortable than a halo, but I really do think that you might have regarded me in a different light from the hysterical ladies in question. You and I used to be friends (intermittently), and though there are one or two details in our past intercourse that might better be expunged, still I don't see why we should let them upset our entire relationship. Can't we be sensible and expunge them?

The fire has brought out such a lot of unexpected kindliness and charity, I wish it might bring out a little from you. You see, Sandy, I know you well. You may pose to the world as being gruff and curt and ungracious and scientific and inhuman and SCOTCH, but you can't fool me. My newly trained psychological eye has been upon you for ten months, and I have applied the Binet test. You are really kind and sympathetic and wise and forgiving and big, so please be at home the next time I come to see you, and we will perform a surgical operation upon Time and amputate five months.

Do you remember the Sunday afternoon we ran away, and what a nice time we had? It is now the day after that.

SALLIE MCBRIDE.

297

P.S. If I condescend to call upon you again, please condescend to see me, for I assure you I won't try more than once! Also, I assure you that I won't drip tears on your counterpane or try to kiss your hand, as I hear one admiring lady did.

The Dochther is ashleep and I can't be lettin' ye oop.

THE JOHN GRIER HOME,
Thursday.

Dear Enemy:

You see, I'm feeling very friendly toward you this moment. When I call you "MacRae" I don't like you, and
when I call you "Enemy" I do.

Sadie Kate delivered your note (as an afterthought).
And it's a very creditable production for a left-handed
man; I thought at first glance it was from Punch.

You may expect me to-morrow at four, and mind you're
awake! I'm glad that you think we're friends. Really, I feel
that I've got back something quite precious which I had
carelessly mislaid.

S. McB.

P.S. Java caught cold the night of the fire and he has the
toothache. He sits and holds his cheek like a poor little
kiddie.

Dear Judy:

Those must have been ten terribly incoherent pages I dashed off to you last week. Did you respect my command to destroy that letter? I should not care to have it appear in my collected correspondence. I know that my state of mind is disgraceful, shocking, scandalous, but one really can't help the way one feels. It is usually considered a pleasant sensation to be engaged, but, oh, it is nothing compared with the wonderful untrammeled, joyous, free sensation of being unengaged! I have had a terribly unstable feeling these last few months, and now at last I am settled. No one ever looked forward to spinsterhood more thankfully than I.

Our fire, I have come to believe, was providential. It was sent from heaven to clear the way for a new John Grier. We are already deep in plans for cottages. I favor gray stucco, Betsy leans to brick, and Percy, half-timber. I don't know what our poor doctor would prefer; olive green with a mansard roof appears to be his taste.

With ten different kitchens to practise in, won't our children learn how to cook! I am already looking about for ten loving house mothers to put in charge. I think, in fact, I'll search for eleven, in order to have one for Sandy. He's as pathetically in need of a little mothering as any of the chicks. It must be pretty dissipiriting to come home every night to the ministrations of Mrs. McGur-rk.

How I do not like that woman! She has with complacent firmness told me four different times that the dochther was ashleep and not wantin' to be disturbed. I haven't set eyes on him yet, and I have just about finished being polite. However, I waive judgment until to-morrow at four, when I am to pay a short, unexciting call of half an hour. He made the appointment himself, and if she tells me again that he is ashleep, I shall give her a gentle push and tip her over (she's very fat and unstable) and, planting a foot firmly on her stomach, pursue my way tranquilly in and up. Luellen, formerly chauffeur, chambermaid, and gardener, is now also trained nurse. I am eager to see how he looks in a white cap and apron.

The mail has just come, with a letter from Mrs. Bretland, telling how happy they are to have the children. She enclosed their first photograph—all packed in a governess cart, with Clifford proudly holding the reins, and a groom at the pony's head. How is that for three late inmates of the John Grier Home? It's all very inspiring when I think of their futures, but a trifle sad when I remember their poor father, and how he worked himself to death for those three chicks who are going to forget him. The Bretlands will do their best to accomplish that. They are jealous of any outside influence and want to make the babies wholly theirs. After all, I think the natural way is best—for each family to produce its own children, and keep them.

Friday.

I saw the doctor to-day. He's a pathetic sight, consisting mostly of bandages. Somehow or other we got our misunderstandings all made up. Isn't it dreadful the way two human beings, both endowed with fair powers of speech, can manage to convey nothing of their psychological processes to each other? I haven't understood his mental attitude from the first, and he even yet doesn't understand mine. This grim reticence that we Northern people struggle so hard to maintain! I don't know after all but that the excitable Southern safety-valve method is the best.

But, Judy, such a dreadful thing—do you remember last year when he visited that psychopathic institution, and stayed ten days, and I made such a silly fuss about it? Oh, my dear, the impossible things I do! He went to attend his wife's funeral. She died there in the institution. Mrs. McGurk knew it all the time, and might have added it to the rest of her news, but she didn't.

He told me all about her, very sweetly. The poor man for years and years has undergone a terrible strain, and I fancy her death is a blessed relief. He confesses that he knew at the time of his marriage that he ought not to marry her, he knew all about her nervous instability; but he thought, being a doctor, that he could overcome it, and she was beautiful! He gave up his city practice and came to the country on her account. And then after the little girl's birth she went all to pieces, and he had to "put her away," to use Mrs. McGurk's phrase. The child is six now, a sweet, lovely little thing to look at, but, I judge from what he said, quite abnormal. He has a trained nurse with her always. Just think of all that tragedy looming over our poor patient good doctor, for he is patient, despite being the most impatient man that ever lived!

Thank Jervis for his letter. He's a dear man, and I'm glad to see him getting his deserts. What fun we are going to have when you get back to Shadywell, and we lay our plans for a new John Grier! I feel as though I had spent this past year learning, and am now just ready to begin.

We'll turn this into the nicest orphan-asylum that ever lived. I'm so absurdly happy at the prospect that I start in the morning with a spring, and go about my various businesses singing inside.

The John Grier Home sends its blessing to the two best friends it ever had!

Addio!
SALLIE.

THE JOHN GRIER HOME,
Saturday at half-past six in the morning!

My dearest Enemy:

"Some day soon something nice is going to happen."

Weren't you surprised when you woke up this morning and remembered the truth? I was! I couldn't think for about two minutes what made me so happy.

It's not light yet, but I'm wide awake and excited and having to write to you. I shall despatch this note by the first to-be-trusted little orphan who appears, and it will go up on your breakfast tray along with your oatmeal.

I shall follow *very promptly* at four o'clock this afternoon. Do you think Mrs. McGurk will ever countenance the scandal if I stay two hours, and no orphan for a chaperon?

It was in all good faith, Sandy, that I promised not to kiss your hand or drip tears on the counterpane, but I'm afraid I did both—or worse! Positively, I didn't suspect how much I cared for you till I crossed the threshold and saw you propped up against the pillows, all covered with bandages, and your hair singed off. You are a sight! If I love you now, when fully one third of you is plaster of Paris and surgical dressing, you can imagine how I'm going to love you when it's all you!

But my dear, dear Robin, what a foolish man you are! How should I ever have dreamed all those months that you were caring for me when you acted so abominably SCOTCH? With most men, behavior like yours would not be considered a mark of affection. I wish you had just given me a glimmering of an idea of the truth, and maybe you would have saved us both a few heartaches.

But we mustn't be looking back; we must look forward and be grateful. The two happiest things in life are going to be ours, a *friendly* marriage and work that we love.

Yesterday, after leaving you, I walked back to the asylum sort of dazed. I wanted to get by myself and *think,* but instead of being by myself, I had to have Betsy and Percy and Mrs. Livermore for dinner (already invited) and then go down and talk to the children. Friday night—social evening. They had a lot of new records for the victrola, given by Mrs. Livermore, and I had to sit politely and listen to them. And, my dear—you'll think this funny— the last thing they played was "John Anderson, my joe John," and suddenly I found myself crying! I had to

snatch up the nearest orphan and hug her hard, with
my head buried in her shoulder, to keep them all from
seeing.

> John Anderson, my joe John,
> We clamb the hill thegither,
> And monie a canty day, John,
> We've had wi' ane anither;
> Now we maun totter down, John,
> But hand in hand we'll go,
> And sleep thegither at the foot,
> John Anderson, my joe.

I wonder, when we are old and bent and tottery, can
you and I look back, with no regrets, on monie a canty
day we've had wi' ane anither? It's nice to look forward
to, isn't it—a life of work and play and little daily
adventures side by side with somebody you love? I'm not
afraid of the future any more. I don't mind growing old
with you, Sandy. "Time is but the stream I go a-fishing
in."

The reason I've grown to love these orphans is because
they need me so, and that's the reason—at least one of
the reasons—I've grown to love you. You're a pathetic
figure of a man, my dear, and since you won't make
yourself comfortable, you must be *made* comfortable.

We'll build a house on the hillside just beyond the
asylum—how does a yellow Italian villa strike you, or
preferably a pink one? Anyway, it won't be green. And it
won't have a mansard roof. And we'll have a big cheerful
living-room, all fireplace and windows and view, and no
McGURK. Poor old thing! won't she be in a temper and
cook you a dreadful dinner when she hears the news! But

we won't tell her for a long, long time—or anybody else. It's too scandalous a proceeding right on top of my own broken engagement. I wrote to Judy last night, and with unprecedented self-control I never let fall so much as a hint. I'm growing Scotch mysel'!

Perhaps I didn't tell you the exact truth, Sandy, when I said I hadn't known how much I cared. I think it came to me the night the John Grier burned. When you were up under that blazing roof, and for the half hour that followed, when we didn't know whether or not you would live, I can't tell you what agonies I went through. It seemed to me, if you did go, that I would never get over it all my life; that somehow to have let the best friend I ever had pass away with a dreadful chasm of misunderstanding between us—well—I couldn't wait for the moment when I should be allowed to see you and talk out all that I have been shutting inside me for five months. And then—you know that you gave strict orders to keep me out; and it hurt me dreadfully. How should I suspect that you really wanted to see me more than any of the others, and that it was just that terrible Scotch moral sense that was holding you back? You are a very good actor, Sandy. But, my dear, if ever in our lives again we have the tiniest little cloud of a misunderstanding, let's promise not to shut it up inside ourselves, but to *talk*.

Last night, after they all got off,—early, I am pleased to say, since the chicks no longer live at home,—I came up-stairs and finished my letter to Judy, and then I looked at the telephone and struggled with temptation. I wanted to call up 505 and say good night to you. But I didn't dare. I'm still quite respectably bashful! So, as the next

best thing to talking with you, I got out Burns and read
him for an hour. I dropped asleep with all those Scotch
lovesongs running in my head, and here I am at daybreak
writing them to you.

Good-by, Robin lad, I lo'e you weel.

SALLIE.